Channing of Concord

Channing of Concord

A Life of William Ellery Channing II

FREDERICK T. McGILL JR.

Rutgers University Press

New Brunswick   *New Jersey*

To my mother
FLORA STODDARD MCGILL

Foreword

Unlike his distinguished uncle of the same name, Channing was a failure, and he knew it. In middle life he wrote:

That is my special function, the having and the being of opacity. Dull I came upon the planet, untalented, the one talent still in that tremendous napkin, out of which I have never been able to unwrap it and where it is still like to be for all I can discern thro its folds.

Still, I shall seek a little longer before I shut up the magic lens called opportunity and utterly hibernate, like the woodchuck whose tracks I do not see all the long winter thro. But every animal makes tracks, only some do not come into view. Why even I succeed in making tracks in the snow, and others in walking in them. Methinks, this is the greatest success I ever had in life.

Why do we bother about a man whose talent was never unwrapped?

The first answer is that Channing was a part of the Concord environment, like the scrub oaks and the gray squirrels. From the summer of 1842 when he knocked on Emerson's door until the day of his death in Frank Sanborn's northwest chamber almost sixty years later, he considered Concord his home. Intimate of Emerson, Alcott, and Hawthorne, brother-in-law of Margaret Fuller and of Thomas Wentworth Hig-

ginson, and day-by-day comrade of Thoreau in travels by
wood and river, Channing wove a bright if tenuous thread
into the curious Transcendental web. Concord's Golden Age
owed much to Channing; and although his own metal was
less precious than gold, it had a catalytic value to his contemporaries.

The second answer lies in Channing's own product in
verse, essay, biography, and notebook jottings. He was the
most prolific contributor to *The Dial*. He was a newspaper
editor, the first biographer of Thoreau, and the author of
seven volumes of verse. His failure in authorship is indis-
putable, but is not absolute. He disappoints us, as he did his
friends, because he was forever falling short of his promise
as Emerson and other well-wishers early conceived it. Channing's contribution to the stream of verse meandered like
his own Musketaquid, apparently careless of its goal, and
often overflowed, so that the channel was lost. Yet occasionally he wrote a good poem, and more often a memorable
line. His *Thoreau, the Poet-Naturalist*, for all its elegiac arti-
ficiality, has proved an important source book. And the unpublished notebooks, in their casual references to his contemporaries, their unpretentious descriptions, and their
flashes of wit, offer a major claim upon our interest.

The third answer is that Channing made tracks in the
snow for others to follow in. When he stated this as his
greatest success, in the journal of 1867, he probably had
literary trails in mind. He may have recalled, for instance,
that his first published poem, "The Spider," had been followed by Emerson's more celebrated "Humble-bee" in the
same jogging meter. But his influence on his contemporaries
was more than literary: particularly on Thoreau, whose
independence, I believe, was reinforced by the friendship,
but whose eccentricities were moderated by the alarming
example of his companion. Furthermore, as a contributing
member of the Transcendental group, Channing can be ac-

corded his share of the credit for bringing a new experimental spirit into the stream of poetry.

Finally, Channing deserves to be remembered as an object lesson in that self-expression that runs wild. The unfriendly critics of Transcendentalism liked to point at Ellery. Lacking the self-discipline of Thoreau, he was less able to carry the heady wine of Emerson's philosophy. Relying on himself spiritually, he was forced to lean on his father and his friends for material support.

Central to this object lesson is the tragic story of his marriage to Ellen Fuller, which their contemporaries regarded as a test case of Emersonian principles. Whether or not it now proves anything about the validity of those principles, at least it seemed to do so then—and that gives the story importance. Channing's uncle, James Handasyd Perkins, who tried unsuccessfully to prevent the marriage, saw in it "the practical results of—what I can only call Emersonianism,—as it presents itself to young minds and hearts." Many, he said, who were inclined to like Emerson's abstractions, "have been shocked by what they thot the concrete consequences." Thus we see in this event, not only an application of these abstractions, but also the attitudes of witnesses to whom Emersonianism was a dangerously radical way of life.

Channing failed as a husband, as a writer, perhaps as a man; but in the course of that failure he achieved some successes. The successes deserve our recognition. The failure warrants our study.

Acknowledgments

So many years have passed since I first began rummaging for facts on Ellery Channing, I can name only a fraction of the scholars, collectors, and librarians who have helped me. Foremost is Ellery's grandson, the late Henry M. Channing of Sherborn, Massachusetts, who opened to me his files and his library without restriction, and who with his brother Walter purchased for my use a considerable body of manuscripts which the Channings later presented to Harvard. My thanks go also to Ellery's great-grandson Laurence M. Channing, who has continued his father's generosity. Another branch of the family has given me permission to use and to quote from the vast Fuller correspondence, now at the Houghton Library. For this invaluable source I am grateful to Mr. and Mrs. Willard P. Fuller and Miss Elizabeth Channing.

It was in Professor Ralph L. Rusk's seminar at Columbia that I adopted Ellery Channing as a subject for research; and one of Dr. Rusk's many contributions was to put me on the trail of those manuscripts that eventually found their way to Harvard. After Dr. Rusk's retirement, the successor to his chair and his seminar, Professor Lewis Leary, proved to be a friendly adviser and guide. A third scholar, Professor Walter Harding, secretary of the Thoreau Society from its inception and editor and biographer of Thoreau, has aided me in countless ways—including a careful reading of my typescript. I am indebted to Mrs. Herbert Hosmer and Mrs. Caleb Wheeler, both of Concord, for contributions to my knowledge of the town as it was in Channing's day. Many thanks go also to Mrs. Veronica Hassold Mach of Nutley, New Jersey, who as an undergraduate assisted this project in its early stages, and filled with painstaking accuracy hundreds of essential note cards.

I am grateful to the following repositories of rare books and manuscripts, and to the individuals who let me use what I needed: The Boston Athenaeum (Mr. Walter Muir Whitehill), the Boston Public Library (Mr. John Alden), the First Unitarian Church of Cincinnati, Ohio (Mrs. Alexander Brown), the Concord Free Public Library (Mr. Edward J. Diffley and Mrs. Marcia Moss), the Harvard University Archives (Mr. Clifford K. Shipton), the Houghton Library at Harvard (Dr. William H. Bond, the late Dr. William Jackson, and Miss Caroline Jakeman), the Massachusetts Historical Society (Mr. Stephen T. Riley), the Pierpont Morgan Library (Mr. Frederick B. Adams, Jr., and Mr. Herbert Cahoon), and the New York Public Library (Mr. Robert W. Hill).

For permission to quote from family letters and manuscript journals, I wish to thank—in addition to the Channings and the Fullers—Mr. Shepherd Brooks (Caroline Sturgis Tappan letters), Mr. John P. Marquand, Jr. (Curzon family letters), Mrs. Ward Thoron (Samuel G. Ward letters), Dr. Eleanor M. Tilton (now editing the unpublished Emerson letters), the Trustees of the Ralph Waldo Emerson Memorial Association, and Mr. Richard F. F. Nichols, who has allowed me to quote from the privately printed *Recollections of Richard F. Fuller.*

For the illustrations, I am indebted to the W. E. Atkinson Company of Newburyport, Mass., the late Mr. Henry M. Channing, the Concord Free Public Library, Mr. Willard P.

Fuller, the Harvard University Archives, and the State Street Bank and Trust Company of Boston. Mrs. Esther Howe Anderson of Concord, Messrs. Theodore and Willis Atkinson of Newburyport, Mrs. Christina M. Welch of Curzon's Mill, and Mrs. Mary Chisholm Sweetser of Malden, Mass., all helped me in my search for the right pictures.

Finally, there are those who had known Channing personally and who later shared their recollections with me. None of them is living today, but I am grateful for the help of Mr. and Mrs. Chilton Cabot, Mr. Herbert Hosmer, Judge Prescott Keyes, Miss Helen Legate, and Mr. Francis Sanborn—all of whom were young residents of Concord when Channing was their elder neighbor.

Contents

Channing of Concord

Childhood

(1817–1834)

Dr. Walter Channing, with a growing practice in obstetrics, kept a methodical record of all deliveries. The entries he made in his "List of Midwifery Cases" were cool and impersonal. In November of 1817 he added to the column:

—29th   Mrs. B. H. Channing   Boy 104

His interest in this case was more than professional, however, for Boy 104 was his own son.

The baby had good blood, distinguished blood, if ancestry was any guide. The Doctor himself was Professor of Obstetrics and Medical Jurisprudence at the Harvard Medical School, after sound preparation at the universities of London, Edinburgh, Pennsylvania, and Harvard. One of his brothers, Dr. William Ellery Channing, was the minister of the Federal Street Church. Another brother, Edward Tyrrell Channing, was Boylston Professor of Rhetoric and Oratory at Harvard. William, their father, whose ancestors were the Channings of Cruxton Manor in Dorsetshire, had been at-

torney general of Rhode Island, and had been appointed
by President Washington to be the first United States at-
torney for that district. His wife Lucy was the daughter of
William Ellery, the Rhode Island "Signer," descended from
Governor Dudley of the Bay Colony and his daughter Anne
Bradstreet, the first New England poet.

The baby's relatives on his mother's side were eminent,
too; here the merchants predominated. His grandfather
Samuel Gardiner Perkins was the youngest of three brothers
who had succeeded to the business of their mother, the
famous "Widow Perkins," and had achieved success in the
export trade. In the 1780's the oldest brother, James, had
established a company in San Domingo dealing in sugar and
coffee; in this enterprise Thomas Handasyd, the second
brother, had joined him temporarily; and in 1785 Samuel had
entered the partnership. The insurrections culminating in
1791 put an end to their business ventures, however; and
after a brief attempt to carry on at Port au Prince, Samuel
returned to Boston and married. Unlike his brothers, who
amassed considerable fortunes in the China trade, he dealt
for a time, unsuccessfully, with India, then turned to the
tamer occupations of selling insurance in Boston and growing flowers as a hobby on his Brookline estate.

Samuel's wife Barbara, daughter of Stephen Higginson,
a powerful Federalist, was a celebrated beauty and wit.
Talleyrand had met her while in exile, and told George
Ticknor in 1818 that she was the most beautiful young person he had ever known.[1] Some of this charm was transmitted
to her daughter Barbara, whom Dr. Walter Channing married in 1815.

Boy 104, in whom these imposing lines converged,
promptly received a special reminder of his inheritance. He
was christened William Ellery—not for his Channing uncle,
but for and at the request of his great-grandfather of that
name, the Signer of the Declaration.[2] Since he had two first

cousins named William, the parents called Boy 104 by his middle name.

Ellery was a rebel, and shook his tiny fist at the universe whenever it said No to his desires. His mother cuddled him, admiring his long, dark lashes, and wished that his beauty could somehow be swapped for a calmer disposition. But between his temper tantrums he was a happy child. He played affectionately with his sister Barbara, a year and a half older, who was irritable but not rebellious, and together they listened to all the stories their parents would tell them. Their father's tales were their favorites, but their mother had more time to entertain them, and she often read edifying little narratives by Maria Edgeworth. When Barbara was five, old enough for school, her mother decided to teach her at home. So Ellery listened as his sister memorized passages from the Psalms, he heard the lessons in *Knowledge of Nature* by Mrs. Trimmers, and he looked over Barbara's shoulder at the maps in Cumming's geography.[3]

The family was growing and prospering. A second daughter, Mary, had been born in 1820, before Ellery was three; two years later came Lucy. Dr. Channing was now the Dean of the Harvard Medical School; his reputation was spreading. Ellery at five could hardly have known what was expected of a Channing or how well his father measured up to it; but he liked the man who took him in his lap for storytelling. When he needed deeper consolation, say for a bruised shinbone, Ellery could always find his mother, whose arms were waiting. It was a warm family, where every need was answered.

Then, suddenly, Barbara Perkins Channing died. This was the end of Ellery's secure little world.

The relatives dutifully offered their help, and Dr. Channing accepted it, feeling wholly inadequate as a single parent. So the family was distributed. Ellery found himself with his Forbes cousins on Milton Hill, in an old house that overlooked the shipping lanes of Boston harbor.[4]

Aunt Margaret Forbes was no stranger to the tall ships that stood out to sea below her windows. The younger sister of Grandfather Perkins, she had married Ralph Bennet Forbes in 1799. Forbes was energetic and deserving, but his every effort in business had been rewarded by failure. Margaret shared his energy and his buoyant spirit, for after bearing six children she followed her husband on a business mission to France in 1812, and with him underwent capture by the British. After their release they reached Bordeaux, where she gave birth to John Murray Forbes in 1813. With the baby they survived battles at sea and a second capture on the way back to America.[5] Now her husband lay dying in the old house, and Margaret darned and patched in her attempt to clothe decently the five young Forbeses who were still at home.[6] At least the new little boarder could pay his way.

Ellery was unhappy. The cousins were all older than he, and needed no more brothers. Perhaps the warmth of Aunt Margaret's nature had spent itself in continual frustration. Long afterwards, in a fanciful mixture of autobiography and fiction, Ellery invented a character named Leviticus, who recounted events of his childhood at Aunt Guthrie's in Templeton, near the salt water. Leviticus recalled being sent to a dame school, but remembered that he had preferred solitary walks to books. "I cannot say," he added, "that I sincerely loved any in my youth; Aunt Guthrie I feared; her reading of religious books I mistrusted." [7]

In the fall of 1824 Ellery was transferred to the Round Hill School in Northampton. This little academy had been founded only the year before by Joseph Green Cogswell and George Bancroft, who were ready to challenge tradition. "We wish to give a practical character to our institution," they said, "and educate not for an ideal world, but for the world as it is. We would make not laborious students only, but faithful and useful citizens." [8]

The curriculum of Round Hill seems severely classical today, and the courses were rigidly prescribed. But the masters set individual excellence as the pupil's target, rather than a relative superiority; and they let each boy advance at his own rate. Punishments were abolished except that the laggard student must finish his work satisfactorily before being allowed to play. The masters trusted their pupils, and shared their activities and interests.

Ellery found that here his ideas were treated with respect, and that he was somehow important. Still he was lonely. He lacked the will or the skill to make friends. Some of the older boys at Round Hill he had known in Boston, and two were his relatives: his young uncle James Handasyd Perkins and his Milton Hill cousin John Murray Forbes. But they were far too old to be companionable. He kept to himself as much as the masters would allow. [9]

Such solitude was limited, for the boys were rarely left to their own devices outside the classroom. As physical development was to keep pace with intellectual growth, the school encouraged wrestling, horseback riding, and other vigorous sports, and required the boys to cut and saw their own firewood. [10] Mr. Cogswell took the pupils on little excursions equipped with geological hammers; and when they had pounded rocks for a while, they would sit down for a short lecture. One project was the construction of a village— "Cronytown" they called it. They snared rabbits, shot partridges with arrows, and roasted their game along with sweet corn for a Cronytown feast. [11] The sunsets, birdcalls, and fragrances of those early years drifted into Ellery's receptive memory, half consciously to be recalled in later life.

At a corresponding period, Leviticus—the semifictional Ellery—attended a "populous *Gymnasium*" swarming with "idle, dissolute boys." He suffered agonizing pains from the colic, but later would recall pleasantly his woodland walks at nutting and sugaring-off seasons. Leviticus had nothing to say about books at this school, but he thought that the intimate acquaintance gained with a broad river and a blue-green mountain contributed to his later love of art and literature.[12]

After Ellery's summer holiday in 1827 he was enrolled in The Classical School in Brookline, where his grandfather Perkins lived. Six years earlier, a group of public-spirited citizens, dissatisfied with educational opportunities in their town, had established this academy for boys and erected a building on Boylston Street in the style of a Grecian temple, with Doric columns. Residents of Brookline took great pride in this architectural achievement—a pride somewhat diminished a few years later, when a spacious dormitory for boarding pupils was attached to the north side of the temple, destroying its symmetry.[13] In The Classical School Ellery was subjected to further experimentation with advanced educational theories.

Sometime in the late 1820's a little girl was taken to the school to witness the effects of "exhilerating gas." The pupils to whom the gas was administered showed reactions which were highly amusing to the audience. The majority became pugnacious, and struck out at their nearest neighbors, including the schoolmaster himself. One boy, John Randall, became sentimental, reclined on the platform, and recited, "Roll on, thou deep and dark blue ocean, roll." The little girl was most impressed by Ellery Channing, who "leaped in the most extraordinary manner like a grasshopper over the heads of the boys on the platform and frightened me sadly lest he should come down on me."[14]

Another glimpse of The Classical School is offered by Charles Sumner, who substituted as an assistant teacher early in 1831 when the headmaster, Mr. L. V. Hubbard, had to make a trip to Vermont. Here is a part of Sumner's report to an old friend:

. . . And oh.—*quorum magna pars fui*—the harassing, throat-cutting mind-dissolving duties; pounding knowledge into heads that have no appetency for it, and enduring the *arguing* of urchin boys, and all those other ills to which schoolmaster-flesh is heir. . . . But the cares of Mr. H's school are more severe than those of most schools, on account of the want of classification in the boys, and the being obliged to drudge through lessons with single boys without any of the excitement of hearing a large class, and also the attention bestowed on them out of school. . . .[15]

Channing was presumably among these boys.[16]

It is possible that he attended the Boston Public Latin School for a short period in 1831; if so, it was for but a fraction of a term, as the school has no record of his enrollment. That year the Master of Boston Latin, Frederic Percival Leverett, resigned his position in order to establish his own school for boys.[17] Two of the Latin School pupils whom Leverett carried with him were William M. Evarts and Henry J. Bigelow. Channing would later recall his close association with both boys;[18] probably he became their schoolmate at this time in the new academy. It was Leverett who "offered" Ellery Channing to Harvard College in 1834.[19]

But Ellery's boyhood was not all schooling. Between terms there were lengthy visits to his father and to the countless other relatives. At Dr. Channing's house there were no chores to usurp his time, for a manservant took care of them. Ellery was free; he might row his little boat on the muddy waters of the Back Bay, or burrow among the bookshelves of the Athenaeum, which occupied his great-uncle James Perkins' old mansion on Pearl Street. He saw something of social life, in Boston and elsewhere. Several times he visited his Aunt Lucy, Mrs. William Russel, in New York. On a memorable trip to Newport, he attended the trial of the Reverend E. K. Avery for the murder of a young woman; he could never forget the villainous look on the face of the defendant.* In other respects Newport was tiresome; his relatives would close the shutters in their library at three in the afternoon, light the tall candles, and sit down to hours of whist.[20] At such times Ellery's loneliness was acute. But there were also visits to other, livelier cousins and cousins-by-marriage, including the Sedgwicks in Lenox and the Curzons in Newbury. In these houses there was movement, and there was young laughter that sounded long after the hour for shutters and candlelight. The loneliness retreated a bit, biding its time.

The Curzons, especially, must have treated Ellery with warm affection before he entered college. Otherwise he would have planned his exit somewhat differently.

---

* Despite his villainous looks, Avery was acquitted. See the Newport *Mercury*, Dec. 29, 1832; May 4, 1833; June 8, 1833.

Triflecut College

(1834)

Channing was admitted to Harvard on September 1, 1834, with a condition in arithmetic. Weighted down by his formidable pedigree, he found in college life no escape from family. His Uncle Edward was the Boylston Professor of Rhetoric and Oratory; his Uncle William, who had been a Fellow under President Kirkland, was now an Overseer, and frequently conducted prayers at Holden Chapel; his father was Dean of the medical faculty. He met his kin even in the street names. On Ellery Street lived his father's cousin, Richard Henry Dana. Just a few weeks before, Channing had waited at the Danas' while Richard Henry Jr., with some difficulty, persuaded his father to let him leave college and go to sea.[1]

Channing went to live in the gambrel-roofed house of the Reverend Abiel Holmes, who had offered the prayer at Dr. William Channing's ordination years before at the Federal Street Church in Boston. Like the brick halls of the Harvard Yard, the house with the gambrel roof fairly breathed New England history. Dr. Holmes said that Gen-

9

eral Artemas Ward had planned the fortifications of Bunker Hill downstairs in the east room. That was the grandfather of Sam Ward, whom Channing had known at Round Hill. In this house General Warren had slept before the battle of Bunker Hill, and perhaps afterwards General Washington. The house offered ample space for student roomers, since the Holmes family was now reduced to three. Of the five children, two had died, one had married, and only John remained at home. The older son, Oliver Wendell, was studying medicine in Paris.

Harvard had long since ceased to be primarily a training school for clergymen; and with the growth of the Unitarian influence and the recession of hell-fire from the students' consciousness, the college was becoming ever more secular in spirit. Yet outwardly the Puritan disciplines remained. Almost every day the Faculty met to pass judgment on boys who had misbehaved. If on a Sunday one wore a brown coat instead of the black or black-and-white mixture prescribed, he would probably be haled before the President for a warning lecture. Let it happen a second time, and he would receive a public admonition. Were he to carve his initials on his bench in Harvard Hall, he might be fined a dollar. But these were the lesser offenses. More serious was "grouping" in the College Yard; serious mischief might come from students who met in numbers and laid their heads together. For grouping, one might get the maximum penalty, which was to be requested to "take up one's connexions"—that is, to leave for good. Serious indeed were all distracting sounds during divine service, such as the operation of squeaking instruments or the cracking of walnuts. For the latter offense, or for such a breach of the peace as throwing snowballs in chapel during service, one might expect to be suspended for a period of months. These were the daily concerns of the Harvard Faculty.[2]

Shortly before Ellery's arrival, two Middlesex County boys

had tried vainly to clear the reputations of two classmates charged with making a noise at prayers. The accused pair were sent away, and warned that if by reason of their appearance in the Yard any "excitements" should occur, the facts would have an influence on the question of their readmission. One of those who tried to be heard in their defense was David Henry Thoreau, who would rearrange his name before becoming famous.[3]

The course of study was as rigid as the rules of Sunday dress. For freshmen it was Greek, Latin, mathematics, and history. Greek included Xenophon's *Anabasis,* composition, grammar, and Greek antiquities. Latin meant Livy—plus composition, grammar, and Roman antiquities. Mathematics was geometry; history required the study of Tytler's *Elements of General History, Ancient and Modern.*[4]

The story of Channing's college career is brief. From the beginning he failed to conform. Family tradition says that he submitted his own curriculum to President Josiah Quincy as a substitute for the program prescribed. True or not, the tale testifies to Channing's perverse individualism and to the influence of his earlier custom-tailored education. But the rigidity of the Harvard curriculum was already under attack, and the act attributed to Channing represents the rebellious attitude of countless undergraduates. Nor were the students alone in their disapproval of Harvard ways. Bancroft and Cogswell, Channing's old teachers at Round Hill, had resigned from the college because of dissatisfaction with its methods. Soon even George Ticknor, the Smith Professor of Modern Languages, was to leave, discouraged by his failure to effect important reforms.*

* Ticknor's resignation was submitted on May 6, 1835, and accepted the next day. But as early as Jan. 5 he had written to C. S. Davies of Portland, Maine: "I have substantially resigned my place at Cambridge, and Longfellow is substantially appointed to

Whatever his desire for curricular independence, Channing was registered in the regular course of study. He resolved to please his father by making at least a show of effort, by filling his room with formidable volumes which should impress the tutors, and by attending enough recitations and chapel services to keep his hold on respectability. But even this degree of discipline was too demanding. The rules of conduct and the grading system humiliated him, for he had grown beyond that level: even in Mr. Leverett's school there were no marks or punishments. Channing quickly concluded that Harvard had no scholars. He found the tutors to be narrow, the professors complacent, the course of study concerned only with microscopic details and quite devoid of poetry.

His attendance was spotty, and as the term advanced he was missing more and more. During the final fortnight, he cut more classes than he attended.[5] Once, after avoiding church on Sunday, he was called in by the President and told he must mend his ways or be put out. He replied that he would do as he thought best.

Under President Quincy, a student's achievement was measured by an elaborate system of points which gave weight to both the quantity and the quality of his work. An apt student might accumulate better than 1,400 in the first marking period. When the grades for the freshman class were figured in early December, 1834, they showed the sum of 1,455 credits for Henry Lawrence Eustis, who had made

fill it. . . . I have been an active professor these fifteen years, and for thirteen years of the time I have been contending, against a constant opposition, to procure certain changes which should make the large means of the College more effectual for the education of the community. In my own department I have succeeded entirely, but I can get these changes carried no further. As long as I hoped to advance them, I continued attached to the College; when I gave up all hope, I determined to resign." (*The Life, Letters, and Journals of George Ticknor*, I, 399–400) a good start toward high scholastic honors. A classmate who had worked less diligently, and who would be penalized again and again before the Faculty yielded his degree, was James Russell Lowell. His score was 1,069. William Ellery Channing II had 554.[6]

On December 4, before the totals had been reported and before the Faculty could sit in solemn judgment upon the delinquents, Ellery "took up his connexions" and found a haven in Newbury with the Curzons, who owned a gristmill—of which, more later. Apparently the departure was an accomplished fact before Dr. Walter Channing received a hint of it.* This was undoubtedly the expedient moment for leaving.

To the Channings, for one of their number to default in this way on his obligations was almost unthinkable. Among the descendants of the Puritans, who still ruled Boston socially, morally, and intellectually, the rule of life was *noblesse oblige*. The doctrine of election had spent its brimstone terrors, but there remained the sense of stewardship to the Almighty Will in those who regarded themselves elected. It was a high privilege to be born into a patrician family; one paid for it by preparing for—and then assuming—the burdens of nobility. That is—unless one was Ellery Channing.

Why was Ellery indifferent to a formal education? Deeply ingrained was the conviction that he was a special case—a conviction that probably had its origin in his family's solicitude. His father wished desperately to act with wisdom; but as every effort to help Ellery seemed to fail, Dr. Channing admitted his helplessness, and Ellery must have sensed his father's discouragement and subconsciously reveled in his

* There is no proof that Dr. Channing had *not* been consulted. But see quotation on page 14 (from "The Youth of the Poet and Painter"), an account which in most other essentials is true to the facts.

importance as a problem child. He had no reason to doubt what his family had always demonstrated by their actions— that for only sons who are also motherless, the world must make special arrangements. His entire life to date had followed an odd curriculum built to match his peculiar needs: Round Hill, Mr. Hubbard's, Mr. Leverett's. Why, he asked, should his existence at this point be narrowed by President Quincy's course of study and rules of behavior? Who would be the educated man at last—Eustis, hunched over Zumpt's Latin Grammar, or Dick Dana, already rounding the Horn on the brig *Pilgrim*? Harvard might serve well enough for one who would run in a groove, but a special nature demands a special freedom.

Whatever the roots of his rebellious personality, there is no doubt about the feelings that they nourished. Ellery himself has told what he thought of Harvard in a series of semi-autobiographical letters called "The Youth of the Poet and Painter," written some years later for *The Dial*. The poet Edward Ashford enters Triflecut College, and after a few unhappy weeks among educated ignoramuses who call themselves scholars, he takes refuge in a gristmill. Whereas Channing was motherless, his fictitious counterpart Ashford is fatherless; but Ashford's mother is as devoted and as baffled as Dr. Channing. When she hears that her son has fled from Triflecut, she writes the boy a letter from the family home in the city of Doughnut:

I was surprised to learn you had suddenly deserted college, and made your way to some place in the country, without either consulting me or the president. As your mother, and nearest living relative, your feelings should have led you to inform me of this very serious change in your course of life. You left Doughnut, apparently contented to reside at college, and President Littlego's first letter was perfectly satisfactory. In his second I was mortified to learn you did not attend prayers, so often as was required, though regular at recitations; and in his third, with what feelings I cannot describe, I learned you had left your room, and the greater portion of your clothes, and taken up your residence at some obscure farmhouse, in a country village. . . .

Hope [Ashford's artist-friend] informs me you pass part of your time in a boat or some old mill. I beg of you not to be out in the evening air. . . . Old mills are badly ventilated.

A letter follows from Edward's sister Fanny, reporting that President Littlego has visited their mother. Fanny writes:

Of all pompous persons he is the chief.*

"Madame," said the President, ". . . Have you received any intelligence from your son Edward since he saw fit to leave his duties? . . . I hope he did not remark in that letter . . . that any too difficult tasks had been imposed upon him by the several departments in college. We treat all the boys alike; the utmost republicanism prevails in our system; and it is impossible that Ashford should have been overloaded with requirements. I am surprised he should have left us, and I am authorized to say by the board of control, that even now, if he chooses to return immediately, he will be permitted to again unite himself with his class." [7]

But neither Ashford nor Channing accepted any such offer. Channing believed it had been childish to go to college, and would have been childish to stay on, once he had seen what it was like. It was now time to put away childish things.

* "Quincy's policy toward the students, an alternate cuffing and caressing, ended in making him the most unpopular President in Harvard history since Hoar. . . . In his conferences with them he was abrupt and tactless, often committing the unpardonable sin of criticizing their dress, or the whiskers which (greatly to his disgust) began to sprout toward the end of his administration." (Samuel Eliot Morison, *Three Centuries of Harvard,* 251)

The Professional Poet
(1835–1839)

Channing was no stranger to Curzon's Mill when he chose it as his refuge on vanishing from Cambridge. The miller was Samuel Curzon, the foster-son of Channing's great-uncle James Perkins; [1] and Mrs. Curzon's brother had married a Perkins. No doubt Channing's intimacy with the Curzon family and their arcadian life had been established in his childhood.

One reached the mill by traveling about three miles west from Newburyport. The road, flanked most of the way by stone walls and level hayfields, began at last to curve downwards, then tumbled steeply through a dark cover of pines and hemlocks. In a clearing at the foot was a two-story farmhouse, and just beyond it a gristmill, gray with time and weather. At the mill, a narrow bridge crossed the Artichoke River.

The Artichoke was a placid stream, and sometimes in the spring the fallen willow blossoms riding lightly on the surface seemed to have no motion. Yet no one could wonder long which way the current ran, for to the right of the bridge and less than half a mile away were the sparkling and energetic waters of the Merrimack.

On the opposite or western bank of this ravine in 1697, the town of Newbury had granted John Emery twelve acres "provided he build and maintain a corn mill to grind the town's corn from time to time." [2] Long before Samuel Curzon's era, the original mill had been replaced by another, on the eastern shore; and it was this that Curzon had taken over, ten years before Channing's escape from Cambridge.

The Curzons had four children: Elizabeth, Mary, Margaret, and George—all younger than Channing. "One of the happiest families I ever saw," [3] Thomas Wentworth Higginson said of them some years later; and it is likely that Channing's poetic eyes found an idyllic picture of domestic affection, well suited to the rustic sweetness of the valley.

Channing was a paying guest (room and board $4 per week) [4] in one of the several chambers which the Curzons rented to their young acquaintances. These rooms included mysterious quarters in the attic of the main house, where stern portraits stared from the walls; [5] and, in the mill, delightful, remote little apartments that trembled with the grinding. [6] But the grinding seems to have been infrequent and ill rewarded; the family economy, precarious at best, relied more upon garden produce, pigs, and chickens. Mrs. Curzon's cousin, the wife of Professor Andrews Norton of Harvard, assisted with gifts from time to time, including among them a carpet and a cow; and she sent her studious son, Charles Eliot Norton, as a vacation boarder. [7]

In the next five years Channing would often enjoy the warm hospitality of Curzon's Mill. In his writings on the Artichoke, the scenes, the people, the incidents, and the dreams of love all coalesce. In reconstructing this winter visit, one may take what he will from "The Youth of the Poet and Painter," remembering that New England's little rivers in December are better for skating than for boating.

This spot combines the attraction of two rivers, wrote Edward Ashford to his painter friend, Hope . . . The larger, in contrast with the less, seems almost a sea, from its high banks. . . . There is a wildness in the larger river, that would better suit you, than my little boating-ground. . . . My little skiff dares not tempt the flow of the large river, and winds its way on the tranquil bosom of the Willow. . . .

Have you been much in a mill? It is a domestic place. There is an honest tone in the spinning stones, the impersonation of a loaf of bread; it is a speech of power besides, rolling and whirling. The beams, coated with dust, glow like dead alabaster, and every spider's web is made from white yarn. Even at noon, the rooms are lit badly, and at twilight they gloom. I am startled when the miller treads the creaking stairs; and the trap-doors and odd passages seem like an old castle. When grinding stops, silence hangs over the chambers, tenanted by squab figures, in white clothes, while down stairs the water trickles under the wheel, and the rats play hide-and-go-seek. Sometimes I am miller, and once I nearly set the building on fire by letting the grist run out of the hopper. . . .

You must come here to paint. They will furnish a room in the mill, where you can hear the hum of the lazy water-wheel, and the owl's screech, out of the forest on the opposite bank. We have good sweet meal, an orchard of scraggly apple-trees, and a deep kitchen hearth for cool evenings.[8]

"The Youth of the Poet and Painter" does not say how soon Channing's baffled father called him home. We know, however, that financial pressures forced Curzon shortly to rent the house and mill, and to take employment in New York. Channing visited the family in their new city quarters during the summer of 1835, and asked wistfully when they might all go back to the mill and be happy again. Curzon tried to persuade him that true happiness springs from doing one's duty, regardless of the place; but the boy did not wholly comprehend.[9]

Except for brief vacation trips, Channing was once more

living with his father in Boston. There are persuasive in-
dications that he had returned home by February, 1835,
for in that month someone began to borrow books on Dr.
Channing's membership—long unused—in the Boston Athenaeum. A dozen titles were charged out in March alone.
Apparently Ellery was observing his new freedom from
formal schooling by a self-imposed curriculum. He may not
have read every book he took home, and perhaps he was
not the only borrower on the Channing share. But it is unlikely that his father or his sisters were now plodding to
the Athenaeum once or twice a week, or that many of the
books were for their use.*

Some of these titles were of legal works. Knowing that
many a lawyer was self-taught, Channing may have seen
in the *Nisi Prius* and in Justinian a solution to his most
urgent problem. Uncle Richard Ashford, in "The Youth of
the Poet and Painter," suggests that Edward may find a
career in the office of Lawyer Smealmin; and Channing may
have determined to sample the discipline on his own. Surely
he felt the need of a positive move to justify himself to
his family, to his friends, to himself.

Judging from the Athenaeum records, Channing made no
eager dive into these legal waters; at first he barely wet
his toes. In February, Gibbon's *Miscellaneous Works* was
charged to the Channings; Chapter 44 of the *Decline and*

* Like many a Bostonian of substance, Dr. Walter Channing owned
a share in the Boston Athenaeum, which was housed in the former
mansion of Ellery's great-uncle, James Perkins, on Pearl Street. The
physician used his borrowing privilege sparingly. In thirty-two months,
from March, 1827, through October, 1829, only forty-four titles were
charged to his account, an average of one every three weeks. In
the next five years, not a single book was drawn on Walter Channing's
share. The period of active borrowing, which began in February,
1835, ended suddenly and for all time in October, 1839—the very
month that Ellery moved to Illinois. See Athenaeum Records: Vol.
I (1827–35) and Vol. II (1835–43).

Fall was required reading at Harvard Law School. In March three law books were borrowed, and no more until 1836, when a dozen were recorded, including *Story on the Constitution* and *Kyd on Awards,* which were on the Law School reading lists. On September 23, 1835, Channing visited a law court, and wrote a verse about a poor derelict of a man encountered there.[10]

It is significant that this courtroom experience produced poetry rather than notes on legal practice. In "The Youth of the Poet and Painter," Edward Ashford decides to be a poet, and it is hard to believe that Channing ever had any other serious desire after the spring of 1835. His mind would play with this vocation and that; it would work upon these vocations after its own fashion, as upon the law in 1836. But if he had entered the office of Lawyer Smealmin, it would have been only in order that the Poet might eat.

To Channing the doors of the Athenaeum were primarily the gates of poetry. There were Klopstock and Goethe—the Teutonic giants who reaffirmed the divinity of the poet—standing mighty, imperturbable as the mountains on which the lightning played in their most awesome imaginings. There was Herder, giving a tongue to the German national energy. There was Bishop Percy, who preserved the British folk-spirit in the ballads of countless bards, unknown but yet divine. Here also were Byron, singing the jagged peaks of Europe and of life; Coleridge, for whom the dreaming was more real than the waking; Wordsworth, the dedicated spirit who made no vows but knew that vows had been made for him: prophets all, with feet on earth, with heads bathed fitfully in the mists; solitary souls whose fellowmen could know them but in part. Nor was all the poetry revealed in verse; there were the exotic fancies of Beckford's *Vathek* and of Ritson's *Fairy Tales;* the wistful confidings of Charles Lamb, city dweller and prose writer, but yet with a poet's soul; and the mixture of sentiment and mischief that was Laurence Sterne. These and others passed through the doors of the Athenaeum—presumably with Channing.

Meanwhile, a new author, one with an unknown name, stole unheralded into print in April, 1835, in the Boston *Mercantile Journal*. This was Hal Menge, whose literary behavior was as odd as his name. By the end of the summer, the *Journal* had printed nineteen of his pieces, nine of which were verse. Six were little essays entitled "Shakespeare," in which the Bard served mainly as a point of departure. One was a fragment of a Gothic tale. One was a review of Whittier's "Mogg Megone." Two were "sketches." These nineteen ran the gamut from rhapsody to clowning. Often there were sudden transitions of mood, as bewildering as if a deacon had turned a cartwheel in his Sunday suit.

Hal Menge was Ellery Channing.

The Gothic tale, "Diavolo," is duly accommodated with squeaking hinges, a screech owl, and clouds scudding across the moon. The inspiration could well be Monk Lewis. Diavolo's victim is forced to dig his own grave. So far, so good—at least, so Gothic. But the final line, whether the author intended it so or not, has a suggestion of the comical. " 'Enter thy grave,' said Diavolo. . . . Then Antonio was seen creeping to his last bed—but he suddenly stumbled and fell headlong into it." With a ridiculous dive, Antonio and the tale come to their undignified ends together.[11]

The review of Whittier's poem opens soberly. "The New England Magazine is rising into the clear sunlight. . . . The poem of Mogg Megone is rhythmical, simple, natural—a narration of startling effect." Suddenly Hal Menge cuts a little caper and brings in a friend with one of the whimsical names that he loves to invent. "Intemperate praise is folly—but after FRIZZLE said to me, 'Whittier hath an indifferent poem in the last Magazine,' I resolved feebly to desire the

Americans to read him, and contradict my worthy friend FRIZZLE." [12]

There can be no valid objection to such whimsy when it serves its purpose; certainly a name like Frizzle might pop up readily enough in Addison or Irving or Dickens. But Channing had not learned to establish a mood and maintain it sufficiently to convince the reader of his sincerity. In the most serious works of art there is often a humor that informs the whole, and is inseparable from the rest of the organism. But Hal's caprices are usually nailed to the outside of the original structure.

In "Paul, a Sketch," he adopts the mannerisms of Jean Paul Richter, but he may have been caricaturing Ellery Channing:

. . . Paul was not what we call a poet, for that name conveys to the reader something remarkable, mingled with an indiscreet, verse-making capacity, fixed in a great, spiritual case, with a pre-eminent will at work, shaping sundry eternal things; now Paul had nothing of this kind, yet he might pass for a true Poet with half the world, for that half makes a Poet something opposite to the opinion above.

. . . The most amazing thing in Paul's career was the unexampled absurdity in which he did all things, realizing in his existence, a monstrous humanity. Never shone the sun on a more amiable being—so modest was he, so gentle, so free from selfishness, so worthy of love; and never shone the sun on a greater absurdity. He crossed the street as others cross, leg after leg, but he had committed more extravagances in those few steps, than three of your common men commit in their lives. Here was his absurdity: he was nothing more or less than a thought-waster. With Goethe he had conversed while in crossing the street; spent an hour in the Vatican; written a Poem or two, after his fashion, and done innumerable ridiculous, fantastic things. He was ever conceiving, never performing, all imagination, nothing of sense. He rackets on in a terrible manner till he finally falls in love.

Love is enough to unhinge the soberest fool—what did it do

with such a fool as Paul? Have mercy upon us if we do not detail his capricios, fandangoes, whisk-abouts, eccentricities, his hurry and worry, now here, now there, soon with the man in the moon,—there can be no possible use of dwelling on the length of his nose—it was always long enough. He was a melancholy fool, of a most quiet appearance, basking in the sun with a musical precision. He did not hoot to the Owls, after the manner of Wordsworth's Boy of Wenander . . . for there was an incessant, original hooting that sounded up from the profundities of his Soul, . . . not to mention his being sovereign, reigning monarch of all Owls, even from farthest time. What need had he of your common, appreciated owl-hooting, when the sound within was like a multitudinous company of musical instruments, playing apparently upon themselves, making his pulses flurry, and his mind a Bedlam, with their infernal sound. Verily, Paul, thy prime minister deserved the patent for owlism, but thou were alone, gigantic, a Cleopatran owl-obelisk, needing no support, no philosophy, no schooling at primary institutes, or primeval colleges,—hooting was thy *self*.[13]

No whisk-abouts or fandangos interrupt the sonnet to Joice Heth, though the verses offer promise rather than fulfillment. Joice Heth was an ancient Negro woman for whom the claim was made that she was 161 years old. When she was exhibited in Boston in September of 1835, the *Journal* carried this advertisement:

JOICE HETH

161

YEARS OF AGE

This greatest wonder of the age, is attracting crowds of ladies and gentlemen at Concert Hall. . . . None can behold her and the document accompanying her, without the most perfect satisfaction that she was the *Nurse of the immortal Washington,* and as old as represented. She is continually cheerful, talking, laughing, or singing, and is a most interesting and pleasing curiosity.[14]

The sonnet is weighted with neoclassical mannerisms, but in the sestet the poet reaches toward freshness and precision, and the tone is consistent throughout:

> Intolerable Time grasps eagerly,
> With hideous Destiny, who sits him near;
> Some name him Fate—it matters not to me,
> So that thy awful durance shall appear.
> Old ebon Heth, eternal Black! Strange sight!
> Strange that thou dost not bend to Father Time,
> But, rather, holdest confident thy prime,
> In this quick-speeding world, where hovers Night.
> Yes, bleached anatomy! Dry skin and bone!
> Thou grasshopper! Thou bloodless, fleshless thing,
> That still, with thin long tongue dost gayly sing!
> I would not meet thee at broad noon alone;
> For much I fear thee, and thy yellow fingers,
> Thy cold, sepulchral eye, where moonlight lingers.[15]

A better poem was "The Spider," which Channing placed in the *New England Magazine* for October. Once more he made the perilous journey to the end—a greater distance this time—without succumbing to the imp within. Perhaps Herder's verses on the dragon-fly had suggested the sprightly four-stress line; * but Freneau, too, had chosen it for his caty-did, and Emerson would follow with his humble-bee.

> Tender of a mystic loom,
> Spinning in my silent room
> Canopy that haply vies
> With the mortal fabric wise . . .
> There are times of loneliness
> When a living thing we bless—

* Herder's poem was in Taylor's *German Poetry*, borrowed from the Athenaeum on the Channing membership on June 16, 1835.

Times of miserable sin,
Cold without and dark within:
Then, old spider, haply I
Seek thy busy factory;
Always finding thee at home,
Too forecasting e'er to roam.
So we sit and spin together
In the gayest, gloomiest weather. . . .

No matter that the monthly which Channing had recently seen "rising into the clear sunlight" was ending its
brief career with this issue. The *New England Magazine*
had published Whittier and others with solid reputations;
now it welcomed Channing. From this moment he knew he
was a poet, and what he proudly called "a professional
poet." *

* Sanborn says of "The Spider": "The success of this early poem
seems to have fixed Ellery Channing's determination to devote himself to literature in the poetic form. In 1847, when, without an
outward vocation, a place was offered him as journalist in a well-
established Boston newspaper, he declined it without hesitation, saying to a friend in Concord: 'I told them that, by the grace of God,
I would never desert the Muse any more, place or no place, poor
or rich; that I would stick fast to her; and that there should be at
least one professional poet left. Twelve years it has cost me to get
here, and what remains shall go the same road.'" (Channing, *Poems
of Sixty-Five Years*, xix–xx)

Lenox and the West

(1839–1841)

For almost five years after leaving Harvard, Channing lived with his father and worried him exceedingly. To Dr. Channing it appeared that the boy had no ambition. He continued to draw books from the Athenaeum, and presumably he read them; but his own production was slight, and his flurry of publication ended July 6, 1836. His cousin William Henry Channing thought him "disposed to insanity." [1] Calling on his reverend uncle, Ellery refused to sit down; when Dr. Channing asked him why, he replied: "Why, Sir, I'm not fit company for you; you are a great man, Sir, and I'm a small one; good morning, Sir." [2] Ellery's father wanted to do his duty, but of what that was he had absolutely no idea.

Occasionally the young poet took off on a solitary excursion. He made such a trip to the White Mountains in the summer of 1836, traveling by stagecoach to North Conway, where he began to walk up the Saco Valley to the Notch. He would remember all his life how a dignified man with white hair overtook him in a farm wagon, and gave him a lift. This was Abel Crawford, for whose family the Notch was named. Crawford took him to his house, seven miles below the pass, and sent him on his way to Tom Crawford's, at the gate of the Notch. Channing passed the Willey house, which only ten years before had been spared by the avalanche when all the Willeys had fled to their death. He took a stagecoach to Ethan Crawford's and Bethlehem, and the Lafayette House, near the Profile; then he journeyed through Franconia Notch on his way home. This mountain trip was but the first of many into the New Hampshire hills.[3]

There was one young man whose society he would have welcomed on such a trip. Recently he had become intimate with Samuel Gray Ward, whom he had known slightly at Round Hill. Sam had been a junior at Harvard during Channing's brief residence there, but the friendship probably developed at Curzon's Mill, where Ward was a frequent visitor, or in Boston, which was home to both men. Ward had bookish tastes, and seems to have lavished on Channing's poems the praise for which the young poet was hungry. Channing guarded this friendship jealously and would gladly have accepted more of Ward's time and attention. As for Ward, he was a normal son of Boston society, with many friends, and had no desire to limit himself to constant communion with a poet, however talented. Yet he had sufficient tact to maintain happy relations with Channing while yielding a minimum of companionship. "Until he met Emerson," wrote Ward, many years later, "I never heard of his having any personal friend but me." [4]

Curzon's Mill offered a surer stimulus to Channing's affections and to his poetic powers than either Boston or the mountains could provide. In 1837 he could return once more to the Mill and "be happy." Particularly in the lazy summer days he let nature work its hypnotic spell upon him and guide his pen, as the *Ariel*, the green and white skiff, drifted idly among the lily pads, or a livelier current swept it past the nooks that the Curzons called Robin Hood's Barn and Titania's Bower.[5] A frequent companion was Caroline Sturgis, two years younger than he—the daughter of Captain William Sturgis, the wealthy Boston merchant. Caroline, like Channing, was a child of whim and gypsy yearnings; to her he addressed many a song of love. Perhaps it was not wholly his fault that she read too much into his ardent rhapsodies.[6] For he was indeed in love, but he knew not yet with whom. Another girl who kindled warm emotions was Mary Curzon, the second daughter—only a child of twelve in 1837, but on his successive visits budding into a most appealing adolescence. Mary was an avid reader, and like Channing could pass in a jiffy from a ridiculous fancy to the most ennobling sentiment—and back again.[7]

Channing was a watercolorist in words. His effects were of the moment and mainly for the moment. Like watercolor sketches, they could seldom be improved by working over and touching up—though he often made the attempt. His forte was spontaneity. He was a true amateur; his love was in the doing rather than in the product. Sometimes his casual verse would give delight, despite a halting line that a counter of syllables would never have allowed. Seldom was there the union of thought and craftsmanship that a critic would call competence. Yet he continually tossed off novel metaphors, both in conversation and in verse; and in his own little circle he won applause for his originality.

But Dr. Walter Channing drew little encouragement from this dabbling in poetry. He finally turned to his brother-in-law, James Handasyd Perkins, for help in solving the problem of Ellery. In the late spring of 1838, Ellery's young uncle was at home in Brookline after six years of vocational groping in Cincinnati. Perkins had exchanged letters with his nephew occasionally; and although he had found Ellery too German—that is, too Transcendental—to be understood,[8] nevertheless he undertook the task of guidance readily enough, feeling a deep sympathy for a boy whose tastes appeared to be much like his own.[9]

On May 29 Channing walked out to Brookline from his father's house, and talked all the afternoon with his Uncle Jim. He had been thinking of studying surgery, he said. (In "The Youth of the Poet and Painter," a fictitious Uncle Richard suggested medical training under Doctor Phosphorus as an alternative to entering Lawyer Smealmin's office.) [10] Now, however, the thought of surgery was yielding to his old love of authorship, though he confessed that he felt no urgings in any direction. On this occasion his uncle thought Channing neither wild nor crazy. Four days later they continued their talk, walking to Nahant and back in order to see Grandmother Perkins. It was a ten-hour excursion, most of it on the road, giving Uncle Jim time to discover his sympathy somewhat lessened with what he called a "misty and unreorganized mind." [11]

Channing was glancing westward. One possibility would be to find work in Cincinnati, where Uncle Jim would resume teaching in the fall. Perkins could hardly contemplate his nephew as a steady boarder; but as a neighbor—well, perhaps. They talked it over with Dr. Walter Channing and planned that Ellery should go to Cincinnati the next spring, taking a room near the Perkinses in Cheviot and sampling the life for a year or so. Uncle Jim expressed faith in the salutary effect of hard work, self-sacrifice, and the influence of Mrs. James H. Perkins. These should bring Ellery to his senses.[12]

Mrs. Perkins was then with her parents in Connecticut, but her husband kept her posted. On June 18 he wrote: "I saw also Walter and Ellery; the latter is all adrift again, is not going with me, is going to Illinois,—no, is not going there but will stay here;—I quit all concern with him unless others cease to interfere."

In the same letter, in an entry dated June 22: "Ellery (since I began this letter) has determined to go to Illinois;—when I write again he will have changed." [13]

The next letter puts a period to Uncle Jim's efforts: "Ellery, as I told you he would, has changed again; his trunk being bought, letters obtained, and funds provided, he thinks he will not go. What is to be done with such a youth? He will neither listen to counsel nor obey command; turn him out of the house and the chance is he would kill himself or become a drunkard; keep him at home and let him go in the old way and he is ruined inevitably. I shall call and see him today and probe his mind, which is, I fear, thoroughly morbid." [14]

The solicitous Perkins may have helped his nephew to reach a decision, but for Channing the main gateway to the West was the Berkshire town of Lenox. Except for the Sedgwicks of Lenox, it is unlikely that he would ever have undertaken an Illinois adventure; and but for his visit to the Sedgwicks' on returning, he might later have steered a somewhat different course.

Charles Sedgwick, clerk of the Berkshire County Court in Pittsfield, presided over the most distinguished household in western Massachusetts—a home in which intellectual brilliance and artistic talent were joined with a heritage of wealth and social position. Charles himself, related distantly to the Channings by marriage, was the son of Theodore Sedgwick, soldier of the Revolution, Congressman, and Associate Justice of the Supreme Judicial Court of the Commonwealth. Charles's sister was Catherine Maria Sedgwick, the novelist, whose books were read even in England. His wife Elizabeth Buckminster Dwight was descended from Jonathan Edwards and belonged to the intellectual peerage of the Connecticut Valley. Mrs. Sedgwick was as much at home in the drawing rooms of Mayfair and the Continent as on her own sunny terrace in Lenox. Their only son, Charles, had by 1839 completed two years at Harvard, leading his class in scholarship and achieving one of the most brilliant records in the long history of the college.* Catherine Maria II, familiarly called Kate, was a musician, already at the age of sixteen giving piano lessons to her neighbors.

To many an eminent visitor from England, American hospitality was exemplified by the Sedgwicks. Harriet Martineau, Mrs. Jameson, Fanny Kemble—all had made their pilgrimages to Lenox, offering their own gifts of beauty or wit to a small circle that could well appraise and treasure them.†

In the late thirties Ellery Channing paid long summer visits to Lenox, frequently staying with the Sedgwicks.[15] Mrs. Sedgwick conducted a girls' school in her own home and had Channing's sister Lucy as a pupil. It is probable, however, that he was drawn there less by brotherly affection than by hero-worship. Charles Sedgwick was one of Channing's idols. Kate wrote of Ellery that "he was always shy and silent, and scarcely spoke to any one but father or mother. To father he showed the devotion of a lover—seeming uneasy whenever he was out of sight, and absorbed in him when he was present." [16]

Kate's mother Elizabeth Dwight Sedgwick also had a strong hold on Ellery's affections, a hold which permitted her to scold him when he needed scolding. On New Year's Day of 1838 he sent her a letter of greeting with a reference to Miss Martineau which Mrs. Sedgwick considered to be in poor taste. She told him so, with some severity. He sent back a message to Lucy, asking her to pay his respects to

* Harvard Term Books, 1837–39. Charles Jr. left college in his junior year because of ill health due, it was discovered later, to a brain tumor. He sailed for Liverpool in 1841, and there took his own life.

† Charles Dickens was there in 1842.

"our kind Mrs. S.," explaining that his letter had been but a frolic for the season, that he had not meant to abuse Miss Martineau, and that in spite of her most severe and bitter epistle he remained Mrs. S.'s "devoted and affectionate pupil."

"From which last epithet," Elizabeth remarked to her husband, "I suppose he means to acknowledge that he has learned a lesson. I was quite touched and softened by the spirit of this message—and think I shall write him again." [17]

Ellery Channing was not the first unsettled youth who had trotted at Charles Sedgwick's side over the Berkshire pastures, or who had sat with him in front of the fire in the Sedgwick library. Mrs. Sedgwick's young brother Josiah Dwight, nervous, moody, long undecided about a career and unsure of his ability to shape one, had found in Charles the combination of stability and sympathy that he most needed. It was Charles Sedgwick who persuaded Josiah in 1838 to leave New York, where discouragement was eating at his heart, and to chop out for himself a livelihood in northern Illinois. From then on, Josiah Dwight was a new man. He wrote back to his niece Kate a series of sprightly letters, exulting in the crude comforts of his log house, delighting in the details of fighting prairie fires, breathing a joy which even a steady diet of salt pork and potatoes could not lessen.*

This was the very year that Channing began to turn his own eyes toward Illinois. There can be no doubt that he was watching Dwight's experiment with eager curiosity. Dwight, like Channing himself, had been adrift; Charles Sedgwick, the idol of both young men, had helped him to get his bearings. When Dwight's reports began to flow back,

* For a full appreciation of how Josiah Dwight's spirits had been lifted, one should read not only these letters to Kate, but also the ones he had written her earlier from New York. All are at the Massachusetts Historical Society.

brimming with self-confidence, Channing could hardly escape the contagion.

A practical handbook for pioneers had recently appeared in Philadelphia under the title *Illinois in 1837*. If Channing read it, he was forewarned on many points. For instance:

Let a man and family go into any of the frontier settlements, get a shelter, or even encamp out, call upon the people to aid him, and in three days from the start he will have a comfortable cabin, and become identified as a settler. No matter how poor he may be, or how much an entire stranger, if he makes no apologies, does not show a niggarly [*sic*] spirit by contending about trifles, and especially if he does not begin to dole out complaints about the country, and the manners and habits of the people, and tell them the difference and superiority of these things in the place whence he came, he will be received with blunt frankness and unaffected hospitality. [Otherwise] he may expect to be marked, shunned, and called in the way of sarcastic reproach, *a Yankee*.[18]

The test of Channing's Yankeeism began in the early fall of 1839, more than a year after Perkins had reported that all preparations had been made for Ellery's journey.* When the departure was imminent, Kate Sedgwick wrote word of it to her Uncle Joe Dwight and advised him, if he met Channing, to cultivate his acquaintance for the sake of his oddity. Joe Dwight took the advice, though perhaps more out of necessity than for the chance of studying eccentricity at close range.[19] For Channing's migration, by canal boat, steamer, and stagecoach, brought him eventually to Dwight's broad acreage in McHenry County.[20] On November 9, 1839, Dwight's neighbors and relatives by marriage, the Griffings, sold Channing three parcels of farm and timber

* The last book withdrawn from the Athenaeum on Dr. Channing's share was taken on Oct. 3, 1839. For evidence that Ellery was the principal borrower, see page 19 and footnote.

land, adding up to a quarter section, or 160 acres. The sale price was $500—more than $3 an acre.[21] Since unbroken prairie had been offered by the government at $1.25 in 1837, it is probable that Channing's land was in large measure already cleared and broken.[22]

The Illinois soil was fertile; Dwight was proving the fact, though gophers, cranes, and wheat rust kept a farmer vigilant. Channing's three tracts were full of promise. The largest plot, of eighty acres, had a gentle roll to it; eastward it leveled off so that one might imagine Lake Michigan out there, thirty-five miles away. The nearest village was Hartland, perhaps three miles distant; but to Dwight it seemed that they were almost a village themselves—this sprouting community of Griffings and Dwights and Channing.[23] They were, however, a small island in the wilderness. They could hear the wolves crying at night from Channing's slew, "like the sharp ringing of small bells."[24]

Channing's little house may have come with the land, or he may have followed the book and called on his neighbors for help in building it. However he acquired the cabin, it had no floor. It was up to Channing to split the yellow poplar, oak, or cottonwood into short, thick planks called puncheons, and to peg them into place.[25] That he never got around to doing it was a measure of his industry. Dwight reported that Channing slept late each morning, but that this was only one hindrance to success. For the rest, "he had no fence, no oxen, no plough, no barn, no wife, and no breakfast, besides having no floor to his house."[26]

While Channing furnished amusement to others, he was himself amused by incidents of the frontier. One night after a session of the criminal court, he helped to bring home the county sheriff in his wagon—the sheriff lying drunk on the floorboards. An inmate of the county jail, remanded to the sheriff's custody, aided in bringing the officer into the jailhouse.[27]

Channing hibernated until planting time—an in-and-out hibernation that let him display his oddities. Then, when the frost was scarcely out of the ground, he was off to the East. In midsummer he returned, but not to stay. Learning from the Dwights that Kate Sedgwick had just landed in America after many months in Europe, Channing back-trailed again, leaving Hartland this time for good. Dwight suspected the reason for this impetuous haste, recalling that Channing had talked much about getting himself a wife.

Uncle Joe wrote to Kate of his suspicions, though not until November, which gave Channing ample time to reach Kate first. "His great mistake," said Dwight, "and the cause of his failure here he attributes to his having bought too much land (160 acres—mine is 325) and I presume if he were to fail in the matrimonial experiment, it would be entirely owing to the lady's having a little too much breadth of foot or length of nose." [28]

By the terms set forth in *Illinois in 1837,* Channing had qualified as a Yankee.

Early in October he turned up once more in Lenox, engaging a room in the town. He had barely brushed the prairie dust from his boots when, to his horror and embarrassment, he encountered his reverend uncle.

Ellery's feelings toward Dr. Channing were a compound of admiration and fear. He respected his uncle's gentleness and modesty, unaffected as they had been by the adulation of thousands. But this mildness of manner sharpened the sting of the doctor's reproofs. Dr. Channing had scolded Ellery before; this time he dressed him down thoroughly for having deserted the West after the family had sacrificed so much to send him there. Ellery was the most irregular of persons, he said. In fact, he was a sinner.[29]

Ellery knew that his uncle was speaking for generations of Channings—and for Perkinses, for Higginsons, for Ellerys, for all the other forebears who had habitually looked down on him from their gilt frames in sad-eyed disapproval. He was sorry to have to disappoint so many, so much, so often.

As soon as he could withdraw politely from this mild but haunting presence, he turned his thoughts to the Sedgwicks, and particularly to Kate. A few hours later, he knocked at the Sedgwicks' door.

To Kate, who rather liked Channing and found his oddities amusing, he was a welcome guest. In his witty comments about Uncle Joe's family, the sheriff of McHenry County, and voyaging by canal boat, she saw a touch of sophistication never before detected. It happened that her father and mother were to pass the next Sunday in Stockbridge and be away overnight, leaving her almost alone, with Grace Ashburner (a neighbor) and the maid. It occurred to her that she would be safer with a man in the house. Her parents joined in an invitation to Channing.

He accepted, and took most seriously his duties as companion and protector. On other occasions he had slighted Kate in favor of her mother and father; this time she received his full attention. They passed Sunday evening pleasantly enough at the piano, singing sentimental ditties to Kate's accompaniment. But, thought Kate, it was just like the old Ellery to slip away the next morning on her father's arrival, without a word of good-bye.

The events that followed may be told best by Kate herself, as she recorded them in her journal:

On Tuesday afternoon, Grace and I met Ellery on the plain. I tho't he looked a little more animated than usual, but as he was never in the habit of shaking hands with any one, I merely said "Good evening, Mr. C" and walked on. Grace sd. to me, "Do you know that you treat that young man in a very cutting manner? I have noticed it sev'l times"—"No," sd I, "I was not aware of it. I am sorry for it, for he needs every encouragement to behave decently himself." In the evg, as we were sitting quietly at work, a knock at the door was answd by Nelly Whitney who bro't in a letter addressed to me, smelling strongly of cigars, and in a hand wh. I did not imme^y recognize. I opened it, and read on for some time without perceiving the nature of it. When I had finished it, I asked Grace for writing-materials, and ran up stairs. A second perusal amazed me even more than the first. He began "My dear Miss S——k, I am certain that I have offended you. Yesterday you treated me as if I were your best friend, this evening you would hardly speak to me, for Gods sake write me instant word how I have offended you. I am in the most terrible agony, suffering more than at the death of my mother. I will here confess what is the interest I take in you—" etc. He then says why confess, since I must know his feelings. He knows that only yesterday I returned his love—do I not remember Sunday evening and the song I sang him—"You cannot deceive me—you cannot trifle with my feelings—" he bursts into sundry passionate and vehement exclamations, rather as if he were thinking aloud than trying to express his thoughts to another, and finally says "I am worthy of you, the extreme fidelity of my affections is enough." He concludes by desiring me to direct to him care of his father—still I was not clear where he was awaiting my answer—and I wrote it at once, not omitting to inform him that I had been completely ignorant of his sentiments, and that I considered myself free from all blame in my conduct towards him. When I went to the village the next morng. I learned that he was gone, so I mailed my letter. Some days after I recd the following letter—an effusion of angry and mortified pride, which pretty much neutralized all my feelings of compassion, and diverted me excessively.

Will Miss S. do Mr. C. the favor not to mention to any one at any period of her life, his having written the letter of Tuesday last, and will she also destroy that letter and this and say nothing of their contents. Nothing but the deepest necessity would have induced him to write this. He is with gt respect Miss S——k's most ob't sert. It is most mortifying to him to be under the necessity of thus troubling Miss S.—

I sent him a line informing him that my father and mother were already aware of what had passed, and that I was sorry he should deem it necessary to request secresy, since he might be sure this matter should go no farther. and so ends this singular correspondence.

Apl. 1841 Not so—for he sent me from New York (where he stopped on his way to Cincinnati) the letter fastened onto the next page—and lately from Cincinnati, another containing no allusion to what is past—and sounding half-crazed.[30]

The letter "fastened onto the next page" has disappeared. Channing himself has left no record of this incident. There seems, however, to be an echo of it in *Leviticus*, that semifictitious memoir which often gives a distorted but recognizable glimpse of the author's own life. While a farmer in Gooseland, Leviticus proposes marriage to a certain Bella, who rejects him. The account continues:

I looked forth, as it were, on a burnt and charred universe. There had been an explosion of the human powder-mill. Away flew the hopes of the heart, that one minute since were so living, and so beautiful, and fell heavy to the earth, dead, broken, mutilated, black, the mere dull corpses of living joys. . . . I was never young again, it may be here added, after this adventure.[31]

Transcendental Peerage

(1839–1840)

Channing was not the first of his generation "too German to be understood." What James Handasyd Perkins called "German" was the mark of the avant-garde. Sam Ward and Caroline Sturgis were among those who spoke the language of this new mysticism. They talked about the reason and the understanding, imagination and fancy, genius and talent, sometimes using familiar words in unfamiliar ways. Often the devotees could be recognized by their dialect. To call these dedicated persons a cult would suggest a formalism which they neither assumed nor desired; indeed, they prided themselves on their individuality. Outsiders, however, would lump them together as Transcendentalists, and many of the Transcendental brethren accepted the label willingly.

If the new movement had a single prophet, it was Ralph Waldo Emerson of Concord, whose beliefs had brought him a remarkable serenity of spirit. A stranger, hearing that Emerson had spent long boyhood vacations at the old parsonage beside the Concord River, might have assumed that he had absorbed tranquillity from that placid stream. The fact was, however, that in those earlier days Emerson had felt singularly insecure. He suffered from weak eyes and weak lungs; he felt no urgent calling to any of the professions. His record at Harvard was respectable, but not brilliant. Rather half-heartedly, he had a go at teaching school; then he drifted into the ministry, mainly because his family expected it of him. He graduated from the Harvard Divinity School, accepted a call to the pulpit of the old Second Church of Boston, and took a wife. But in his professional duties he was unhappy; he found that he could not perform sincerely all the rituals of the church. In the midst of his spiritual perplexity his young wife died; he resigned from the ministry; and his health broke. At the age of twenty-nine he was thoroughly sick in body and spirit.

But he still loved life, and he had a questioning mind. He knew he needed some kind of new experience. Especially he wanted to know more about a fresh brand of idealism that had sprung from the German philosophers and was being propounded in Britain by Samuel Taylor Coleridge. Another interpreter of the Germans was Thomas Carlyle, a young Scotsman who hated all sham and pretense, and wrote in a style as craggy as the coast of Scotland. Emerson knew he must talk to these men. So he found the money to buy his passage to Europe and back, and enough additional to take him calling on the writers and thinkers whom he most admired. He came back to America, a few months later, virtually a new man, and with a confidence in his own powers he had never felt before.

A short time after Emerson's return, he and his mother settled down for a winter in the old Concord parsonage with his step-grandfather, Dr. Ezra Ripley. Concord was an ideal spot for a man like Emerson, who wanted to read and write. He responded to the beauty of his surroundings in a little book entitled *Nature.* In this essay he expressed the fundamental idea that was to permeate all his utterances from this time on: that through all of nature, including man himself, there flows a divine spirit which constantly reveals new truth to those who seek it. This was more like the Quaker doctrine of the "inner light" than like anything preached in the Unitarian and Trinitarian churches. It was contrary to the generally accepted philosophy of John Locke, who said that all knowledge comes by way of the five senses. This emphasis on the spirit was not exclusively German, of course; Emerson had read widely, and *Nature* showed reflections of Plato, Plotinus, Berkeley, and the Orientals. He drew them all into his statement of confidence that although the external world both delights and serves us, we carry in our hearts all that is essential to the good life.

Emerson was an agnostic in reverse. Most agnostics have a Lockean respect for the evidence of the five senses. They say, "The one thing I am sure of is that this solid earth under my feet exists. I cannot say whether God exists or not, and there is no way of finding out for certain." They may add, "I will assume there is a God, for in doing so I have nothing to lose."

Emerson was a different sort of doubter. To him the one certainty was God, Mind, Spirit, Soul. He questioned whether the world had any independent existence outside the mind. Yet he loved nature, and was enough of a pragmatist to live as if she had reality. "I do not wish to fling stones at my beautiful mother," he remarked.

In 1836, having stabilized his inner life, Emerson sought a new stability for the outward man. He married Lydia Jackson of Plymouth, and bought the big white farmhouse that stood at the end of the Cambridge Turnpike, across town from the parsonage. The next year he wrote a poem for the dedication of a monument at the Old North Bridge, in which he mentioned "the shot heard round the world."

Then he fired two shots of his own that would reverberate beyond the limits of Massachusetts.

The first of these was in 1837, when he addressed the Phi Beta Kappa Society at Harvard. The title of the address was "The American Scholar." With stirring eloquence he urged the younger generation of scholars to declare their intellectual independence; to respect the wisdom of the past, but not to worship it; to seek new truth by communing with nature, reading books wisely, and participating in the life of their time. To the older scholars who heard him, he seemed to have too little regard for the great books of the past; but to the young men his voice was a trumpet call.

The next year he addressed the graduating class in the Harvard Divinity School. Again he spoke of continuing revelations; he insisted that God had not exhausted his truth on tables of stone or in a single divine book. In begging for a newly inspired ministry, he echoed the message of Paul: "For the letter killeth, but the spirit giveth life." The young men took his words to heart, but the professors resented the suggestion that their churches were growing stagnant; and he would not be invited back to speak at Harvard for thirty years.

On October 3, 1839—the month of Channing's Illinois adventure—Emerson sat in his Concord study and acknowledged receipt of a poem. He had been postponing this letter from day to day, for writing it was something of a chore. He wished to thank, to admonish, and to encourage, all at the same time. As a gentleman he must show gratitude, for he was the subject of the verses. As a critic he must recognize that the grammar was grotesque. As a seeker after genius he must respect the latent promise of better verses to come.

He was not addressing the poet directly, but the poet's friend Sam Ward, who had forwarded the lines. He said in part:

I write so slowly I believe because I liked the message so well
& was willing to wait for a select hour to reply to what took
my fancy with the most agreeable surprise. Certainly your
friend in these lines & in the very few others of his that I have
seen, goes to the very end of the poetic license, & defies a little
too disdainfully his dictionary & logic. Yet his lines betray a
highly poetic temperament and a sunny sweetness of thought &
feeling which are high gifts; and the voluminous eloquence of
his Spenserian stanza is by itself an indication of great skill &
cunning.[1]

The day that Emerson wrote this letter, the poet in question was borrowing from the Athenaeum Jewett's *Foreign
Travel*—the last book he would withdraw before departing
for the foreign land of Illinois. A suggestion with which
Emerson closed his letter—that he be given an opportunity
to meet the poet—must wait for another year. But Sam Ward
soon offered Emerson a further sampling of Channing's
poetry, and this persuaded Emerson to initiate an acquaintance by letter.

On January 30, 1840, Emerson wrote to Channing:

Your friend Samuel G. Ward, whom though I have known
but a little while I love much, has communicated to me a number
of your poems which I have read & still read with great delight.
I have seen no verses written in America that have such inward
music, or that seem to me such authentic inspiration. Certainly
I prize finished verses, which yours are not, and like best, poetry
which satisfies eye, ear, heart, & mind. Yet I prize at such a
dear rate the poetic soul, that where that is present, I can easily
forgive the license & negligence the absence of which makes the
merit of mediocre verses; nay, I do not know but I prefer the
first draught and to be present at the secret of creation before
the vamping & rhetoric are used which are but "the brushers of
noblemen's clothes." . . .
Next Spring or Summer, probably in July, we are to have a
new Journal of better promise than any we have had or have

in America; of which Margaret Fuller is to be the Editor. I have promised her my best assistance to write & to collect for her. And I have no plan so much at heart as to secure these poems for publication. I ask you to give me liberty to select some of these pieces & print them in her Journal. I think if you shall permit it, I could easily accompany them with a running commentary in prose that would shade the abruptness and fragmentary character of several pieces & give them due perspective. I feel my dear Sir, that the pleasure I take in this poetry fully authorizes me to make this request. My quarrel with our poets is that they are secondary & mimetic but you may thank the god for intuition & experience. . . .[2]

There was no immediate reply to this cordial invitation. Writing to Margaret Fuller two months later, Emerson listed Channing among possible contributors, but asked, "Where is his answer to my letter?"[3] Not until June, when Channing had returned to Boston, did Emerson receive a note yielding the permission he had asked; even now it was granted on condition that the poet's name be withheld. "So we dear souls must seal our six or eight lips,"[4] said Emerson to Margaret. He tried with Ward's help to arrange a meeting with the poet; once he called at Dr. Channing's house, hoping to find Ellery in—but without success. Suddenly the elusive youth was off once more for Illinois.

Emerson's article "New Poetry," which appeared in the October *Dial*, incorporated twelve of Channing's poems. The casual reader, noting the friendly and hopeful comment, could hardly have suspected how Emerson's fingers had itched to smooth the meters and improve the rhymes. But Margaret exercised her authority as editor of *The Dial*, and six other lips joined hers in urging Emerson to respect the Word as written.

He complained to his neighbor Elizabeth Hoar: "All my conjectural emendations of our wonderful Manuscript Poet came back to me dishonored. Raphael [Sam Ward] and

Margaret combined against me. I think the poet has given them philtres that they (and I believe thou also, O faithful sister mine) do face me down with his bad grammar and his nonsense as all consecrated by his true *afflatus*. Is the poetic inspiration amber to embalm and enhance flies and spiders? As it fell in the case of Jones Very, cannot the spirit parse and spell?" [5]

To Caroline Sturgis he wrote: "What is this Ellery that I, by the acknowledgment of you, of Margaret, and of Ward, a Laureate Critic and Dictator on Rhymes, am unable to hint that this slip of a boy has misspelled a word or omitted a semi-colon, without arousing the indignation of you all, yes and of Elizabeth H. also." [6] There were apparently not three pairs of lips, but four, combined against him.

In his published comments, Emerson recognized the flaws in the versification, but minimized their importance.

They testified that the writer was more man than artist, more earnest than vain; that the thought was too sweet and sacred to him than that he should suffer his ears to hear or his eyes to see a superficial defect in the expression. . . . Here is poetry which asks no aid of magnitude or number, of blood or crime, but finds theatre enough in the first field or brookside, breadth and depth enough in the flow of its own thought. Here is self-repose which to our mind is stabler than the Pyramids. Here is self-respect which leads a man to date from his own heart more proudly than from Rome. Here is love which sees through surface and adores the gentle nature and not the costume. Here is the good wise heart which sees that the end of culture is strength and cheerfulness. Here is poetry more purely intellectual than any American verses we have yet seen, distinguished from all competition by two merits—the fineness of perception and the poet's trust in his own genius to that degree that there is an absence of all conventional imagery. The writer was not afraid to write ill; he had a great meaning too much at heart to stand for trifles, and wrote lordly for his peers alone.[7]

With the appearance of this article, Channing knew that he was enjoying distinguished patronage. And was not Emerson both patron and one of those peers for whom Channing was writing? If Emerson was his peer, then he must be Emerson's. His dedication to the Muse, five years before, was surely vindicated. Only a year before, when he left for Illinois, he was still on the periphery of Transcendentalism. He had not yet met Emerson. He had read widely, however; particularly translations of the German romantic poets who expressed the new religion of the heart. He had absorbed *Nature,* and admired Emerson from afar. He knew that Emerson was controversial, and on the side of all sensitive souls, as contrasted with the businessmen of State Street. He felt the electricity in the air: the excitement of what some were calling "the Newness." He knew about Amos Bronson Alcott, older than Emerson but young at heart, who had been forced to close his Temple School. The parents of Alcott's pupils had objected to his Socratic method of teaching the Gospels, and to his admitting a Negro girl to his classes. Channing saw in Alcott a man who was guided by his inner voice, undaunted by social pressures. Lately he had heard rumors of other noble ventures. There was Brook Farm, a new land of milk, honey, and self-development, into which George Ripley was about to lead his Transcendental band. Now, suddenly, he found himself thrust into the swift current of "the Newness," propelled by Emerson, Margaret Fuller, and *The Dial.*

Channing knew that this was his world, and that already he was committed to it. This—as well as Kate Sedgwick and antipathy for farming—brought him back to Massachusetts. It was most reassuring, as he abandoned the plow, to be accepted as a man of letters.

Ellen

(1840–1841)

Channing was soon to meet in Cincinnati a young lady who looked very much like Kate. She was Ellen Kilshaw Fuller, also from Massachusetts—like Channing groping for security despite the prominence of her family name and the concern of well-intentioned relatives.

Ellen was a child of Timothy Fuller. She was of a restless brood, who were forever on the move. But as one by one they ventured far from Cambridge and Groton, they still remained a family—linked by deep affection, common memories, and their mother's tireless pen. Ever since 1835, when their Congressman father had been laid to rest in Mount Auburn, the Fullers had bound themselves each to each by a web of correspondence, with Margaret Crane Fuller, the matriarch, at the center. The radial strands of this network would eventually reach from the Charles River westward to the Mississippi and eastward to the Tiber, with Mrs. Fuller relaying week after week the homely details of daily living that her children might have failed to write to one another.

In the year 1840 Sarah Margaret, the oldest of these children, was beginning her "Conversations" in Elizabeth Peabody's bookshop on West Street, Boston. To a widening circle she was simply Margaret, her first name forgotten, her last name unnecessary. Eugene and William Henry, the next in age, had already set themselves up in New Orleans as forwarding and commission merchants, with a warehouse in Cincinnati as a way station. Richard and Arthur were still preparing for Harvard—one at Mr. Weld's school in Jamaica Plain, the other with Mrs. Ripley in Waltham. James Lloyd, slow-witted, the youngest of the Fullers, would soon become a pupil at Brook Farm, with just enough wit to know how to vex the older philosophers.

There remained Ellen, the blonde, fragile, middle child, who still must find her proper path. "Truly lovely,—apparently a lover of the flowers," wrote Theodore Parker after meeting Ellen on a June day in 1839. Her life had been close to garden and orchard. In Groton her mother had bordered the walks with flowers, and as a joke her father had cultivated his own little bed of dandelions. Near the piazza of the old white house had stood Ellen's own crabapple tree, some of which was grafted with a particularly sweet fruit, which her brothers sampled at their peril.[1]

Ellen was, in part, the product of these natural beauties that had surrounded her. The love shared by her brothers and her sister had been formative, too. Yet with the sweetness of her upbringing had been combined a severity of discipline. Her brother Richard could remember, years later, their father's firmness on two points: the children must get up early, and they must stick to their bargains.[2]

Beside the talents of her scintillating sister, Ellen's own gifts seemed to herself as middling as her position in the family. It was Margaret who had taught Ellen for long years when the younger girl had been too sick to go to school; how painful the contrast of minds to Ellen—perhaps to both!

Angelic though she looked and often acted, it is no wonder that she was irritable, that her temper seemed her foremost enemy. None felt as much as Ellen Mother's hovering and anxious presence: to Mother she was "dear Ellen," "poor Ellen," "poor, dear Ellen." [3]

Her mother was not the only one to sympathize. Richard, though four years younger, suffered the same consciousness of inferiority under Margaret's tutelage; and he and Ellen were constantly drawn together. Long afterwards, he wrote:

On one occasion when the seriousness of my feelings made me shun a gay conversation, and I secluded myself the better to indulge them, Ellen sought me out and told me she felt for me and with me. She was four years older than myself, a beautiful girl with light ringlets playing around her pure white brow. Her deep blue eyes were full of sympathy, and we shed a few tears together of that "repentance which needeth not to be repented of." I think I did not afterwards refer to this incident; but I never forgot it, and it made me thankful not only on my account but on hers. [4]

Yet the Fullers, including Ellen, admired self-reliance; and as the family fortune dwindled, Ellen set teaching as her goal. In 1837, when Arthur had approved of this ambition, his mother had said: "I do want to give her a few months' good schooling. Sorry to have you say she should teach school, when you are unacquainted with her fitness. However, schooling will help if she *has* to teach for a living." [5] In 1840 that critical moment had arrived. The Groton house had been auctioned, and Mrs. Fuller was safely lodged with Margaret in Jamaica Plain. Ellen was eager to venture forth on her own. The Reverend James Freeman Clarke, the Unitarian pastor in Louisville and Margaret's close friend, was probably the one who made her project possible.

In October of 1840, the month of Ellery's rebuff in Lenox, Ellen debarked from a riverboat in Louisville on her first bold enterprise. She was to live with the family of George Keats, the brother of the late poet, and a leading merchant in the youthful city.*

Sick when she arrived, and "threatened with ague and fever," Ellen was in no mood to fall in love with her new home. She was repelled by the pigs and cows feeding in the filthy streets; the best stores looked to her like the worst in Boston. By turns she regretted her adventure and resolved to make the best of a bad situation. "I have been here about three weeks," she wrote to Richard, "and have seen a good many people, but not one who is worth the trouble of a description." She promptly belied her statement with an admiring account of young John Keats, one of the sons, "full of fun and jokes but withal kind and gentlemanly, as brave as a lion, so the boys say—always fights out all the quarrels of the school." Though Ellen disliked his brother Clarence, she could share with both boys their excitement over the coming "illumination," when the Keatses would join with other citizens in lighting their houses to celebrate the Whig victory. But Richard may have read between the lines that for all the candles Louisville would be Louisville still.[6]

---

* "One of the best men in the world," Clarke had called George Keats in a letter to Margaret (James Freeman Clarke, *Autobiography, Diary, and Correspondence,* 107). Keats was intelligent, too, and well read. Writing to Emerson in 1838, Clarke had said: "My chief companion in the study of Carlyle is George Keats, a brother of the poet. . . . He read 'Nature' with much pleasure, but told me that the song 'Take, oh take,' which you ascribe to Shakespeare, was from 'Rollo,' by Fletcher. . . . 'Sartor' he likes much, and says that often when debating with the other bank-directors about discounting, etc., he is puzzling himself to find out the meaning of what they are all doing by the application of the Sartor philosophy, to tear off the shows of things, and see their essence." (*Ibid.,* 121)

If there was any prospect of teaching immediately, Ellen's maladies destroyed it. A bilious fever in December left behind a rheumatic affection which lingered through the winter despite the ministrations of Mrs. Keats and her daughter Emma. Mrs. Fuller, having decided to do some traveling herself, was then visiting her merchant sons in New Orleans. When she learned about Ellen's plight, she longed to fetch her to Louisiana, where the warm sun and a mother's care should work a cure. Then, she thought, they would embark for Boston by the ocean route, to avoid the expense of land travel and the reckless speed of the river boats.[7]

When William Fuller sailed down the Ohio in January, returning to New Orleans from a business trip, he persuaded the captain to tie up for a few minutes at the Keatses', hoping that Ellen might be taken aboard for the journey south. The girls were abed as William ran up to the house; but Emma modestly concealed herself behind a screen in order that brother and sister might confer. Ellen, he learned, was suffering from recurrent paroxysms which made travel unthinkable. William did what he could: he left a bank draft for $100, which would pay Dr. Edward Jarvis for his attendance and cover some other expenses. He urged her to follow him when she could, and ran down to the boat, which was tugging impatiently at Keats's pilings.[8]

Despite fits of homesickness, Ellen was not yet ready to give up her bid for independence. She had already remarked that she might take a school with James Perkins in Cincinnati when she recovered.[9] Now the invitation to New Orleans offered another prospect; once her health returned, she might take pupils there, rather than surrender her ambitions.[10] Dr. Jarvis, who had known a similar case of neuralgia cured by Louisiana sunshine, encouraged her to make the voyage; and late in February Ellen, still in pain, was helped aboard the *Grey Eagle*.[11]

To Mrs. Fuller, the reunion in New Orleans brought both

joy and grief. Any exertion out of the ordinary renewed Ellen's paroxysms and made breathing difficult. "I consulted Dr. Kennedy about her," Mrs. Fuller wrote to Arthur; "he examined her chest, and thinks the right lobe of the lungs slightly affected, and evidently thought her tendencies consumptive. I intend to have the electro-magnetic power applied as soon as Dr. K. returns from Havana. William Henry thinks we had better move northward the first of May if Frances [William's wife] is able to travel as we hope she will be. We now think of going to Cincinnati by steamboat, stay and rest, go to Pittsburgh by steam, take the canal boats and get home as best we can." [12]

The sunshine in and about the Vieux Carré brought Ellen partial relief, and by early April she was ready to strike out on her own once more. Back in Louisville a teaching assignment was waiting for her—with the children of a Mr. Labue and those of the Baptist minister Dr. Hall, at whose parsonage she might live.[13] As success seemed likeliest there, Ellen took the boat for Louisville on April 3.[14]

In addition to the physical improvement, Mrs. Fuller had noted in her daughter a development of personality. "I have had the deep joy to see my dear Ellen recovering her health, to see her struggle against nervous irritation, and to exercise only gentleness and love; after so much suffering coming out *more* patient, affectionate, and bright from the ordeal." [15]

It was disappointing to Ellen to learn on her arrival at Louisville that Dr. Hall had resigned his pastorate because of disagreement with his parishioners. Fortunately there was still Mr. Labue, and Ellen seems to have moved to his house at this time. But more exciting to Ellen than Halls and Labues was Emma Keats's engagement to Philip Speed, a gentleman farmer. Ellen's letter to her mother so bubbled with the details of the match that there was no word of the neuralgia.[16]

At the end of May, Mrs. Fuller stepped from a river-boat at Louisville and passed eight sweltering days with Ellen. The heat which Dr. Jarvis had prescribed three months before had now settled heavily under the low ceilings of Ellen's chamber and school room, leaving the girl exhausted and— as it seemed to her mother—almost without hope. Yet Mrs. Fuller's visit had its rewarding moments; she found Mr. and Mrs. Keats very polite, and "dear Emma very affectionate and attentive to me." [17]

She would, therefore, have been shocked and puzzled, could she have read the letter which George Keats addressed on July 4 to James Freeman Clarke, who was now settled in Boston at the Church of the Disciples. Keats reported that Emma was now happily married, but that the wedding was accompanied by "one alloy" which he must convey to Clarke in confidence. It was a quarrel between Emma and Miss Ellen Fuller, so severe that Miss Fuller had declined to attend the wedding, had failed to call on Emma afterwards, and had rebuffed Emma's attempts at reconciliation. The cause was Miss Fuller's pique at not having been consulted on the match and not having been "invited in a sufficiently special manner." So far as Keats could tell, it was wholly Miss Fuller's fault.

This rupture, said Keats, was the climax of half a year of tension. He continued:

I never conceived of a girl making so many daily sacrifices (for 6 or 8 months) to gratify the wants and whims of another, as Emma for Miss F. Her conduct was such that Father, Mother, and Sister had ground to believe themselves entirely disregarded. It would not become me to detail the thousand occurrences in which Miss F forced upon poor Emma the performance of divided duties. Everything that her Mother or Georgiana wished her to do Miss F begged, entreated, stormed, and shed tears to prevent her from doing. She ridiculed our acquaintances, found fault with dresses, discouraged the performance of all social duties by trying to prevent a return of visits, shed tears in streams to prevent Emma from going to parties given to celebrate her return home and in fact threw a damp over the family reunion so completely by the ingenious and acute management of her influence over Emma, that poor Emma was worried to a careworn appearance, and in every respect except an occasional burst of hearty feeling totally unlike her former self. She is now herself again; against all rule of etiquette she called on Miss F. since her marriage, was treated rudely, and now I hope all ties are broken between them. . . .[18]

All this was unknown to Mrs. Fuller; and if she wondered that Mr. and Mrs. Keats were no more than polite, no hint crept into her letters. Long before July 4 she had moved on to Cincinnati, heard James Perkins preach in the pulpit just vacated by William Henry Channing, Ellery's cousin, dined at Mrs. Stetson's with the Perkinses, and taken ship once more, eastward and homeward.[19]

Through July Ellen lingered in her stuffy room and kept her little school. She supplemented the three R's with music lessons; and when out of class, she brushed up on her French by reading the modern writers.[20] Though not discouraged, she was far from happy. She was troubled over being the least talented member of her family. She was unquestionably lonesome since her exile from the Keatses'. And she still found it hard to approve of anything she saw. On July 27 she wrote to Richard:

There is to be an exhibition at a girls' school here on Friday evening to which I am going; they have acted before and enjoyed it. I do not like the idea of girls showing themselves off at all, especially in this western country, they are already too forward. They go about the streets without bonnets, and speak to anybody they like, this takes away very much from that withdrawing modesty which makes a woman lovely.[21]

Early in August Ellen and her scant possessions sailed upstream. She was headed for home, where she and her mother might rent a house for the winter,[22] and she could once more enjoy the society of young ladies who wore bonnets. But she stopped off in Cincinnati, perhaps to visit Mrs. Stetson for a few days. One wonders whether Ellery's uncle James Perkins, who also set a high value on "withdrawing modesty," immediately saw in Ellen a woman who would teach by example as well as by precept. Swayed no doubt by his respect for the other Fullers and by a recognition of his need and hers, he was quick to propose that they pool their efforts. Her decision was prompt, for on August 13 the Cincinnati *Gazette* carried this notice:

TO PARENTS

The subscriber will re-open his school on Monday September 6th. His rooms are now on McFarland street, between Elm and Plum. He will hereafter have one class of children under ten years of age, to be instructed by Miss Ellen Fuller, from Boston. Miss Fuller will also give lessons in French and Music.

Any persons wishing their children to join the younger class, will please apply to No. 12 Vine street near Third, between the hours of ten and one, where particulars may be learned.

J. H. Perkins

Perkins' occupations, past and present, were varied. They had this in common—none had produced much income. In less than a decade, Perkins had practiced as lawyer, merchant, editor, free-lance writer, nursery gardener, social worker, teacher, preacher. Overflowing with public spirit, he had crusaded for more and better schools, had served as secretary and trustee of Cincinnati College, had been a co-founder of the Society for the Promotion of Useful Knowledge and of the Cincinnati Astronomical Society. He was one of the editors of the *Western Messenger* in its six years of precarious life.[23] He was still giving time to many of these interests; but there were two principal commitments, to which the school added a third. He had been, since 1838, the agent of the Relief Union, a charity for ministering to the needy which had been established after the panic of 1837. He was also the minister of the Unitarian Church. In the spring of 1841, when William Henry Channing had resigned his pastorate, plagued by the abolition issue, the church had immediately called Perkins to the pulpit.* Although Perkins disliked slavery, he was not an avowed abolitionist, and he seemed a likely candidate to hold together the factions of a divided parish. He had accepted the charge, with the understanding that it would be temporary.[24]

Moderate though he was in his attack on slavery, Perkins was regarded as a social radical even among the Unitarians. In 1840 Harm Jan Huidekoper, the founder of the Meadville (Pennsylvania) Unitarian Church and the Meadville Theological School, wrote to his daughter: "In your last to me you ask me to overlook Mr. Perkins' locofocoism in favour of the good he does. . . . Age and experience will cure Mr. P of his democracy. It is the disease of the young and the theoretic." [25]

Not the least of Perkins' peripheral responsibilities was the wise guidance of his nephew Ellery. The younger man had turned up in Cincinnati in the spring of 1841, accepting the invitation which his Uncle Jim had extended more than two years before. Again Channing tackled the study of law,

---

* On June 24, 1840, the members of the church voted on whether to allow the Cincinnati Anti-Slavery Society to hold a meeting in the church building. The petition was denied, 30-12, with one member "indifferent." W. H. Channing, who was still the minister, voted in favor; Perkins voted against. (Records of the First Unitarian Church)

procuring a desk in one of the local offices, and proving to himself during the summer months that his talents must lie elsewhere.* Meanwhile he did not confine himself to study. One of his first ventures was in journalism: in early April, after President Harrison's death, he was invited to write the long obituary notice for a local paper—probably the *Gazette*.[26] As Harrison had been a Cincinnati man, the assignment had special importance. Also Channing sampled social work. He often accompanied his uncle to the homes of the indigent, and earned or appropriated Perkins' title of "minister-at-large."

"By the way what *do* you think Ellery is doing in Cincinnati?" Kate Sedgwick wrote to her father in April. "He is *minister-at-large*, at least so Mrs. Geo. Minot told me—the girls [Ellery's sisters] declared they did not know at all what he is doing tho' he writes them much oftener and more affectionately than he has ever done before—whereat they are greatly pleased.

"Was there ever such a queer brain?" [27]

Channing made some social calls, also—enough to earn a report that he was "quite a beau." [28] On the surface, at least, he had thoroughly recovered from the Sedgwick affair. Even though, like Leviticus, he might never feel young again, he could appear more lively than ever.

The parents whom Perkins had addressed in the *Gazette* were slow to respond. As the public schools were well established, and there were already forty-four private schools in this city of fifty thousand, perhaps it is no wonder.[29] A week after the *Gazette* announcement Perkins wrote to William H. Channing: "Ellen F. is still with us, I fear she will hardly find a class. She is downhearted and uncertain. . . . We are all pretty mournful. . . . Everyone is poor and hope-

* "Ellery is now in a law office but he dislikes that profession and thinks he has no talent for it—so he will soon give it up." (Mary Channing to Kate Sedgwick, Sept. 21, 1841)

less almost." But between these doleful tidings was a casual sentence which suggests that Ellen's spirits were responsive to the proper stimulus: "Ellery she is decidedly impressed with." [30]

Ellen was certainly looking upon life in the West with renewed interest. Margaret wrote her mother on August 31:

> I have a letter from Ellen, the best I have ever read, I shall show it to you as soon as you come. She has a prospect of being able to stay in Cincinnati this winter where she will make friends and get that experience that may make it worth while for her to have gone out. She seems reconciled in the way of true wisdom. She says, tell Mother that, if it could have been right I should have so loved to see her, but still we shall sometime meet and it is all for the best. [31]

There was more, but nothing that could have prepared Mrs. Fuller for the shock that was to come. It was Channing who confirmed on September 5 what may already have been rumored.

My dear Mrs Fuller

You have probably heard that Ellen is engaged to me. We were to have been married a week from tomorrow, but E. has wished to postpone our union till we hear from you. We are not rich in the world's goods, but I consider myself better off in the love of Ellen, than were I master of 10,000 a year; she is so sweet, fearless, and true. *I have found what I have longed for these twenty years—a home.* Now may the floods beat, now may the winds rave, and the great sun himself be eclipsed, for I have found what I wished, and it is impossible for anything which is considered unfortunate, to harm me any more. Ellen, I think has the deepest, surest, strongest character I have ever known. She loves me so much, so deeply, so truly, that I feel, *a homeless wanderer so long,* in her arms that I am under the shelter as of a wide-spreading tree. . . . It is evident to everyone, that we were made for each other. . . . To you, also, another child has come, one who brings to you, not fame, not influence, one unknown to the world, poor, ignorant—only to be thought of by you as the one loved by your Ellen. Let us, then hear your voice sound to us, (for it is a voice we long to hear), telling that you are glad Ellen has loved and has loved me, for I will be to you, as one of yours, with every respect,

Yr aff.
W E Channing Jr [32]

Some days later, but before the wedding, Channing wrote to Ellen's sister Margaret:

I have read today your letter to Ellen. . . . I am very grateful to you for this sympathy. Though my nature is indifferent to most, I trust it will turn towards you with affection. Indeed, I love but the fewest, and most eagerly forget those I have once known. Less, as I have grown, do I find in my companions to love, more fickle do I become. . . . Few can even like me, yet fewer love. . . .

I am not absorbed in Ellen—it is no exclusive, excluding interest, I am turned to others with kinder feelings; I am desirous of doing all justice; sitting in the warmth of her gentle, generous and friendly nature I feel glad to come out. But it must take many years, to bring me there. . . . I cannot promise you anything, any sympathy, any affection. Your nature may fall upon mine gently, and be pleasant, or otherwise. It is not for me to say. The letter has quite charmed me. . . .

I feel a kind of assurance that all will be well with us. Ellen is so good, I think she will propitiate the fates. Stern is the decree which says to the Poet, thy songs shall bring thee no bread, but this is well, else we should have factories for writing verse. We must yield to the other laws. Is there anything beautiful in us, let it bear fruit. I do not speak of the practicals. I believe Ellen has spoken of those. She cannot misrepresent them. Of poverty, no lies can be told. There it stands, cold, true, and yet with a kind of grin on its face. I smile back to it. . . .

Then Ellen added a postscript:

A letter from Ellery's Father full of kindness both to me and him, has made me very happy. He will help him on this next year and seems full of kindness towards me. I think now that we shall marry as we propose this next Friday—it seems best on all accounts. Be with us then, dear Mother and Sister.[33]

Margaret wrote her reply on October 3, the anniversary of Sam Ward's marriage and his birthday also. This friend "for many years seemed born for cheer and companionship to me, the fair child of my hopes." Ward, she said, had so often quoted Ellery's verses and praised his insight that she had no doubt as to her own feelings toward her new brother. She continued by parrying Channing's brash overtures with deftness and grace:

You say you cannot promise me anything nor tell how my character shall affect you. I had not thought of this for, of a nature which the observer may call vain and presumptuous or affectionate and trustful at his pleasure, it never occurs to me that those I am inclined to love may not receive me till they themselves suggest it. But now I do think of it, there may be much you cannot meet. My character and life have been of various strain and mine is now in a sense a worldly character and one of many sides. You may not like or enjoy meeting me, and I shall not set my heart upon it. It will, however, be easy for me to bear it, if you do not, as I have been long trained to all forms of separation, and I shall not prize you the less. Should you prove the wise and faithful guardian of my sister's happiness . . . you will have conferred on me a benefit, beyond requital, and only to be answered in prayer.

I still think more of Mother than myself in reference to Ellen. . . . This has been a great shock to Mother for it was an event so important in time and eternity that those at a distance felt as if all was done too hastily, and the thoughts of all that it might lead to thronged too fast upon a mother's heart.

Yet we all feel a greater degree of clearness that you have
taken your mutual destiny so decidedly in your own hands; we
wish to trust your inward leading which has spoken in tones
so determined. . . . I have written as to my brother, yet I do
not know whether the vow has been pronounced in the sight
of man.[34]

Channing was essentially sincere, in spite of the hyper-
bole of his letters. At the moment he was wholly committed.
He wrote without reserve because there were no reservations
in his love. The egotism, the bombast, and the bravado were
pure Ellery Channing. Fortunately there was more to Channing than these letters show; but what they reveal was basic.
However theatrical he sounded, he was playing no one but
himself.

One of his statements in the letter to Mrs. Fuller—"It is
evident to everyone that we were made for each other"—
could hardly have been farther from the truth; yet Channing
may have believed it at the time of writing. It was too early
for the protests that were to arrive from Massachusetts. As
for the Perkinses and the little circle of Cincinnati friends,
one must assume that they displayed the utmost tact at
first, hoping that these lovesick youngsters would change
their minds before it became a matter of duty to oppose
them.

That Perkins finally expressed himself is beyond doubt,
as is the fact that he advised them in vain. The ceremony
was performed on September 24 by the Reverend Henry
V. D. Johns, rector of St. Paul's Protestant Episcopal
Church.[35] Perkins, though filling the Unitarian pulpit, was
not an ordained clergyman with authority to perform mar-
riages; their choice of an Episcopal rector was not in itself,
therefore, a sign of Perkins' displeasure. However, that he
and others were displeased is revealed in an unhappy letter
to William H. Channing:

Your letter, which came a day or two since, came too late;
Ellen became Mrs. Ellery C. on the 24th ulto. She did it, however, in opposition, not only to all of us,—but to her mother,
sister, his father and (I fear) her own coolest conscience. Her
course here has probably destroyed her hope of success here.
She came with a strong feeling in her favor. I am sorry to say
that she is by no means popular among those who should have
been her best friends. For my own part I cannot go on connected with her as a teacher, for I have not confidence in her
as a guide to young girls.* I say it to you, (and I trust you
will not suffer even Julia to see what I write,) that to me she
has appeared fearfully wanting in the first of womanly qualities,
modesty. Nor is it to me only; our very domestics have been
critics of her conduct in this regard. I may see the thing un-
fairly, but to me it seems that Ellen is now suffering the practical
results of—what I can only call Emersonianism,—as it presents
itself to young minds and hearts.—She has felt a divine inspiration to marry Ellery, and at once; she has tho't it true womanly
virtue to act out her feelings and impulses,—not to thwart her
nature; and the result is before us.† To others the thing has

* Perkins elaborated on this in a letter of June 12, 1842, to W. H.
Channing: "Some of my severest trials were connected with E. F.;
never have I felt so uncertain as to the right course nor suffered
more from adopting what I deemed the wisest. . . . I was convinced that Ellen's influence was such as made it out of my power
to say to parents that I thought her a proper person to take charge
of young girls; I was also convinced that she was acting against me
in such a manner as would leave me no alternative but to separate
from her or abandon my own school. Under these circumstances I
told her we had better part, and, at her pressing request, I told
her my objections to her. After thus treating her I thought it right
to leave her to act as she pleased with respect to visiting us; and
telling her that I did not wish any coolness to prevent our continuing
as usual on terms of acquaintance, left her to act as she pleased. . . .
Her marriage had nothing to do with the matter." (Massachusetts
Historical Society)

† On June 17, 1842, Mrs. William Minot of Boston, whose son
William Jr. married Kate Sedgwick, wrote to her husband: "While I
was at Lenox, Mrs. Charles Sedgwick received a very good letter

borne the same aspect, and many who were inclined to like your friend's abstractions, have been shocked by what they thought the concrete consequences. I am sorry to say these things, but never have I been so disappointed and never have I suffered so much in two months as since she has been with us. They have now gone to board at the Blackwells'. . . .

The school did not succeed.[36]

The young Emersonians had been faithful to their inner voices. Their friends could only hope that the voices had spoken wisely. "Since all is now decided," Margaret wrote to her mother, "we will look upon the future with hope and trust that the tears with which it is stained are but dewdrops in the morning of a golden day." [37]

from her brother Josiah Dwight at the West. He is at the same place Ellery Channing went to and began with no better prospect except for the difference of character, a difference for which perhaps they were neither of them accountable. It however determined the destiny of each. Mr. Dwight is contented and prosperous, has a good wife and children, and is every year seeing increased daylight in his affairs as well as his forests. Probably his sensible, practical wife has some share in his success. Mr. Dwight says that when Miss Fuller was advised to consult her friends before accepting E. Channing, she replied that she need not take this step for she had a call from heaven to develope Ellery's beautiful character. Mr. D. adds that he found very little of the beautiful in Mr. C. while he was with him, but thinks he (Mr. D.) might have had a call from the opposite (of heaven) to develope the opposite." (Massachusetts Historical Society)

The Golden Day

(1841–1844)

Channing might "smile back" to poverty, but he knew that to smile was not enough. He must face what he called "the practicals."

In his present radiant mood, he was willing to strike a compromise with the ideal; yet he wished to approach that ideal if possible. The good life, as most progressive minds seemed to agree, combined agriculture and poetry in some such blend as at Brook Farm, which Channing had visited early that year before returning West.[1] He and Ellen now considered joining that community. The marriage of intellectual and manual labor seemed an exciting topic among the Unitarians, whether on the Charles River or on the Ohio; and for the Channings the interest was heightened by personal ties. Ellen's youngest brother—Lloyd, the slow-witted—was already at Brook Farm, as a student; and both Margaret Fuller and William Henry Channing were close observers of the West Roxbury experiment. There was even a chance that William Henry, now unsettled since giving up his Cincinnati pastorate, would join the Ellery Channings in establishing a new community.[2] Hearing that the Curzon farm might soon be offered for sale, Ellery wrote Margaret for information;[3] on the banks of the Artichoke a poet might once again find satisfying refuge. These projects danced in his head while he sought in Cincinnati a more immediate solution to his economic problem.

In November he found something that dissipated all thoughts of agricultural communism. It was a subeditorship on the Cincinnati *Gazette*, with a promise from publisher J. C. Vaughan of $400 a year.[4] With this expectation of regular income, the Channings laid plans to set up housekeeping in the spring. They decided also to invite Mother Fuller to share their home. Although marriage had raised Ellen's spirits, she still pined for familiar faces—the more because she was plagued by frequent illnesses. Therefore at the end of the year she dispatched a plaintive appeal to her mother to come West—and to bring furniture. In due time an acceptance arrived: Mrs. Fuller would start out when spring made traveling safe.[5]

As the winter wore on, it brought gradual assurance to the New England relatives that Ellen had, after all, found happiness. On January 8, Margaret wrote to her mother:

I have a letter this week from the two Es of Cincini which I will send you next oppor[y]. All well,—Ellen is to sit for her picture with part of the money the Wards sent her. I shall be glad to have one of her at this time of loveliness and happiness.[6]

And on February 5:

I cannot help feeling much encouraged about them by these letters, though I do not wish to encourage hopes hastily. But Ellen does seem very sweet, equable, and really satisfied, and four months of close communion have passed now.[7]

They took a small house at an annual rental of $200, with space in the back yard for a little garden, and paid $110 for furniture. Channing had no intention of staying with the *Gazette* beyond the fall unless his salary were raised, but he hoped for an increase to $700. He reasoned that if the increase never came, they could sublet the house and get back at least $75 on the furniture.[8]

The subeditor was busy. The *Gazette* claimed his days; at home he alternated between household chores and scribbling. Moreover he determined, now that he was ordering his chaotic life, to collect the many verses which he had for so long been scattering among his friends. He would do this, not for immediate publication, but as a tangible evidence of industry. Eventually he might put a selection from them before the public. He recalled a poem entitled "The Mariner of the Lakes," once presented to Mrs. Ripley; there were several sonnets entrusted long ago to Caroline Sturgis; there should be some odd lines of his in the desks of William Henry Channing and Sam Ward. He wrote to Margaret asking her to collect such of these as she could, and to send them West by her mother.[9]

To his sister-in-law he directed also a stream of musings on literature and life—a shallow stream which sparkled and gurgled and danced. His puns tumbled over one another shamelessly. When Caroline sent him a copy of Bailey's *Festus,* he shot at Margaret a volley of playful comment, asking her to write him "a parcel of little botched, jerking sentences about it. None of that elegant criticism which I don't understand. Send me something deep and strong— mustard-like."[10] He tried himself to be sharp, piquant, as if there were too much sweet writing in the world.

To these letters Ellen wrote postscripts dealing mainly with the practicals, and with messages of love to the members of her scattered family. In her writing she never chortled or whooped, as her husband did; but she sometimes smiled sympathetically. "We had a grand Convention of Tee-total-lers here a fortnight since," she wrote to her brother Richard; "but the poor fellows when marching in the Procession, looked so pale and thin, that I really wanted to offer them 'a drop of something.'" [11] Ellen had humor, but it was not madcap.

At the end of April, Mrs. Fuller arrived in Cincinnati, anxiously seeking the first glimpse of her son-in-law; hoping for rather than expecting pleasure from the acquaintance. She was agreeably surprised. She found a modest, hard-working young man, who stacked the firewood in the kitchen before breakfast and managed other household chores; who departed punctually for the office; who took delight in fetching home fresh vegetables from the market; who bravely accepted poverty and did not scorn to wear mended garments, yet gave generously whatever was his to give. Poor as he was, Channing had hired a man for half a day to prepare a garden for the precious seeds that Mother had brought from Massachusetts. Busy as he was, he found time to do many little kindnesses for the comfort of both Ellen and her mother: to read to them, to converse agreeably. The more Mrs. Fuller saw of him, the more she was impressed by his energy, his courage, and his principles. [12]

Four housemaids had come and gone before Mrs. Fuller's arrival. "It is almost impossible to get a decent servant without high wages here," Ellen wrote to Margaret. [13] (This acceptance of poverty seems not to have been accomplished at one stroke.) So mother and daughter busied themselves in the house and in the little "Massachusetts" garden throughout the forenoons, and after luncheon exchanged calls with their few acquaintances: the Blackwells, the Greenes, Mrs. Walker, Mrs. Ernst, Mrs. Stetson.

Unhappily, James Perkins continued to stand aloof. His coldness troubled Mrs. Fuller deeply; only the June before, when she had passed through Cincinnati, the Perkinses had been most cordial. Now she must avoid the Unitarian church to escape embarrassment.[14]

As spring advanced, and Channing completed his sixth month of work for the *Gazette*, the great question appeared to be not whether his salary would be increased, but whether he would be paid at all for half a year of labor.[15] The answer is unrecorded, but early in July he packed his bags and left for the East. "He was pale as marble the morning before he left home," wrote Mrs. Fuller, "but commanded himself thoroughly after he decided to go. His Father wrote advising him *against* leaving the West the morning everything was ready for his departure. He does not know *how* to advise Ellery—and I hope he will find wise heads to aid, and true hearts to sympathize, and cheer. We thought it best to continue housekeeping, and keep open an avenue to his return if he cannot do better." [16]

Once again a trip east coincided with a burst of recognition in *The Dial*. Not that Margaret as editor had wholly spurned his verses in the interim. Since October of 1840, when he had received Emerson's blessing in "New Poetry," Margaret had published five of his poems before becoming his sister-in-law, and another poem in January, 1842. But it was no coincidence that the July *Dial*, carrying seven poems by Channing, was the first issue under Emerson's editorship.

Emerson still had but the barest acquaintance with Channing. The two had finally met in December, 1840, after Channing's second return from Illinois.[17] But the older poet was eager to know Channing better, and now welcomed him cordially, even giving him a temporary room while Channing sought an inexpensive lodging for the winter.

On August 5 Margaret wrote from Cambridge to Richard Fuller, then at Groton School:

Ellery is here, he wants to see you. I have had one pleasant visit from him. He thinks he shall board at Concord with Ellen, and employ himself at writing through the winter. He has written for Mother and Ellen to come on early in September.[18]

That same day Nathaniel Hawthorne, master of the Old Manse, recorded: "Few indeed are the mortals who venture within our sacred precincts. . . . Mr. Emerson comes sometimes, and has been so favored as to be feasted (with a gnome, yclept Ellery Channing) on our nectar and ambrosia."[19]

Margaret soon arrived at the Emersons' also, hoping to help her new brother in his quest.[20] One possibility which she offered to explore was the Old Manse itself—that venerable parsonage where Emerson had written *Nature*. Channing warmed to the prospect of boarding with the Hawthornes, who were also newly married. Nor were the couples altogether strangers; Channing had met Hawthorne at Brook Farm the year before, and Dr. Walter Channing was not only a friend of Sophia Hawthorne's family, the Peabodys, but one of the many physicians who had tried to cure Sophia's headaches. It was to her that Margaret made the proposal: would she and Mr. Hawthorne consider sharing their living space with a pair whose interests would be so congenial to their own? Sophia gave no indication of her own feelings, but said she would talk it over with her husband.

Hawthorne's letter to Margaret is a model of diplomacy:

Had it been proposed to Adam and Eve to receive two angels into their Paradise, as *Boarders,* I doubt whether they would have been altogether pleased to consent. . . . You will not consider it impertinent if I express an opinion about the most advisable course for your young relatives, should they retain their purpose of boarding out. I think that they ought not to seek for delicacy of character and nice tact and sensitive feelings in their hosts. . . . They will be able to keep their own delicacy and sensitiveness much more inviolate, if they make themselves inmates of the rudest farmer's household in Concord, where there will be no nice sensibility to manage, and where their own feelings will be no more susceptible of damage from the farmer's family than from the cattle in the barnyard.[21]

Hawthorne wrote this letter on August 28. It accomplished the feat of refusing the request without injuring the sensitive Channing, for five evenings later Ellery knocked at the Manse to ask for aid of another sort. While in Cincinnati he had written a little essay entitled "Sundays in the City and Country," which had appeared in the July issue of the *Boston Miscellany of Literature and Fashion.* He had lately been told that Hawthorne was to succeed to the editorship of the *Miscellany,* and wished to discuss that publication, no doubt hoping to open an avenue for regular contributions. It was a vain errand, as Hawthorne never became editor; but it inspired some comments in the latter's notebooks on the "originals" whom Emerson was forever seizing upon as geniuses. Hawthorne was tolerantly amused by the young eccentric; by the fact, for instance, that Channing was seeking to sell columns of prose, but would consider it profanity to accept money for his verse. He was likable enough, Hawthorne thought, though the type inclined to become wearisome. "An innate perception and reflection of truth," he noted, "give the only sort of originality that does not finally grow intolerable." [22]

One man at least had already found in Channing glimmers of universality. In the untamed wit, the spritely antics, the fantastic whims of this child of nature, even in the maddening carelessness of his verses, Emerson saw immortal youth, and he paid homage to it. The spontaneity, the eternal surprise of Channing's remarks, the very independence of convention which made his poems in Emerson's eyes great though not good—these qualities produced the ideal gypsy-comrade, the fellow vagabond of the woods and fields. Through August they walked together, and talked of Greek mythology and knives and forks, of politics and Mr. Rice's shop. They could even be silent together without embarrassment.[23]

As the two poets ambled in the glow of a remarkable sunset on September 1,[24] Ellen and her mother were embarking on their journey east, having auctioned some of the furniture and packed the rest for shipment. Ellen was eager to join her husband, he impatient to receive her. Together with money and much advice, he had sent her a plea to come directly to Concord; only if she *required rest* was she to stop with her mother at Aunt Abi's in Canton.[25] Ellen arrived safely, but they were not to remain in Concord after all. Unable to find suitable quarters, they resolved to postpone the search until spring, and to pass the winter months in Cambridge.*

A letter from Hawthorne to Margaret Fuller, dated February 1, indicates that Channing's visits to Concord were infrequent. "I have missed Ellery Channing very much in my skating expeditions," he wrote. "Has he quite deserted us for good and all? How few people in this world know how to be idle!—it is a much higher faculty than any sort of usefulness or ability. I do not mean to deny Ellery's ability for any sort of vulgar usefulness; but he certainly *can* lie in the sun." [26]

Among the friends whom the Channings visited more than once that winter were Sam and Anna Ward. In 1840 Channing had learned regretfully of Ward's engagement, fearing that the new tie would end the old friendship between them. However, Ward's feeling toward Channing was never so exclusive as to be affected by marriage; and Anna,

* Probably they spent the winter with Margaret on Ellery Street.

who was one of Margaret's intimates, was most cordial to the younger couple.

On December 10, 1842, Emerson noted in his journal:

A good visit to Boston, and saw Sam Ward and Ellery to advantage, and my Parian sister. Ellery has such an affectionate speech, and a tone that is tremulous with emotion, that he is a flower in the wind. He says he has an immense dispersing power. Ward is wise and beautiful and said and admitted the best things. He had found out, he said, why people die: it is to break up their style.[27]

On some such occasion as this, Ward decided to increase Channing's "dispersing power," or at least to open a valve for its release. He would pay for the publication of those verses that his friend had lately been assembling. No doubt Ward shared Emerson's belief that the poems would really speak to an audience of but a hundred or so; yet this hundred would be worth reaching. "Poetry for poets," Emerson called it, seeing in the manuscripts a storehouse of chaotic treasure which others might sometime fit into acceptable patterns.[28] Late in the spring the collection was ready for the publisher.

"When the rudder is invented for the balloon, railroads will be superseded," said Emerson with sagacity. The balloon was Channing's genius, in need of steering apparatus. So far the poet lacked a worthy aim, played fantasies merely, continually broke faith with the intellect, with the reader, with himself. Emerson made these comments in his journal after helping to put together the fragile little volume.[29]

In the meantime, Channing's friends continued to search for a house in Concord. It was another of Emerson's "originals," the earthy Henry Thoreau, who finally acted as broker, securing the little red farmhouse on the Cambridge Turnpike, adjoining Emerson's garden, for $55 a year.[30] There was enough land to challenge the muscles of any poet, and a charming prospect opened on every side. Thoreau himself was about to leave for Staten Island, to tutor the children of Emerson's brother William; but it gave him pleasure to know that in his place would be another lover of the woods and fields.[31]

The golden day of the Channings reached its noon with their removal to Concord in April, 1843. Life there was supremely quiet. Channing reported to Margaret that four carts passed in a day, and two gentlemen "in red faces and bundles, just to keep us from forgetting there are other towns." [32] His principal duties were in the garden, but he often helped Ellen by building the fire, roasting apples, boiling eggs, and washing dishes.[33] At odd times he fished with Hawthorne, walked with Emerson. In the evening were books and pen and paper. "The old world lolls its tongue sleepily," he said; and, responding to the languid mood, he felt a deep contentment.[34]

Elizabeth Hoar was one who saw at the Red Lodge an ideal expression of bucolic simplicity. She wrote to Richard Fuller:

One day this week Madam Emerson and I took tea at Ellen's house and I was charmed with the house, with all its arrangements and Ellen is graceful enough both in herself and her tastes to make a ruder dwelling fair to see. Then they have a blue unbroken dome under the centre of which they stand and look out upon beautiful summer sunsets and sunrises. . . . The way in which our poet lives there with his wife, is more attractive to me, more full of moral and social significance, than any of these communities where simplicity is artificially practised, and goes straight to my heart as none of these ever will.[35]

Channing's newly acquired serenity may account for the mellow tones of "The Youth of the Poet and Painter," the semiautobiographical work already mentioned, which appeared serially in *The Dial* beginning in July, 1843. It took the form of personal letters, half narrative, half exposition, humorous and often slapstick in method but with the serious intent of exposing stuffiness, both in and out of Harvard. It will be recalled that when Edward Ashford, the poet, runs away from Triflecut College and takes refuge in an old mill, his mother begs him to reconsider, for "old mills are badly ventilated." But his tolerant uncle is more of a philosopher. "Do what you like," says he; "only be careful to go to sea with a rudder. I rarely give advice, but I can recommend you never do anything without seeing where your path goes, and, if you can, keep the old road. You will find the beaten path pleasanter, on the whole, and, if the scenery is tame, the accommodation is good at the taverns. . . . What we shall resolve, I cannot say; in the meantime I puff my pipe, at my leisure, in the garret, and read some old French plays I bought at a book stall." [36]

The spirit of caution is most sympathetically embodied in this fictitious Uncle Richard; yet he was the invention of the incautious Channing. There is no doubt that what was safe and tame appealed to one side of Channing's nature. These letters, like the dialogues and "conversations" which he was to write in later years, gave him an opportunity to argue with himself.

The little volume *Poems* appeared shortly after the Channings had moved to Concord. The publication made no stir in the literary world, but Channing's immediate audience was as appreciative as it was small. Early comments, all from friends of the poet, show criticism generously tinctured with friendship. Thoreau sent word not only that he had read the poems with interest over and over, through and under, but also that he had seen a man at Little and Brown's *buy* a copy.[37] Elizabeth Hoar took her volume to bed with her, thinking to glance at a few old favorites before dropping off to sleep, but could get no rest until she had heard all its haunting music.[38] Emerson, who had already dipped his pen more than once in Channing's behalf, wrote an approving notice for *The Dial*, declaring the poet's genius to be in certain respects unrivaled in this country.[39]

But for the real test it would be necessary to wait.

Concord during that May and June was an amusing milieu for a humorist ready to be amused. There was Nancy Wiser, the schoolma'am, who justified her name when she withstood the pleas of the school committee and refused to return to face the offspring of the Irish railroad builders.[40] There was Emerson's latest genius, a native of Concord named Ball, already a remarkable linguist, poet, and novelist though a Ball of only twenty years' rolling, whom Emerson threatened to roll toward the Red Lodge.[41] Within reach of Concord was other rich entertainment—the dedication of Bunker Hill Monument, for example, with Webster's oration, in and out of which Washington stalked, "like a ghost, . . . candle-like, . . . a ghost reading the latest newspaper." [42] There were reports from the various camps of Transcendentalism: such as the news that William Henry Channing was "trying to breathe life into a monthly, to be called 'The Present' "; whereupon Ellery remarked that from the title he inferred it was gratis, and also that it would soon be called "The Past." [43] All in all, Concord and the world which spun around it were a constant delight.

No doubt much of Channing's contentment was rooted in a sense that here was at last a society to which he belonged. Having always been out of step, he found satisfaction in a group where being out of step was fashionable. Emerson was a heretic; yet people bought his essays and listened enraptured to his lectures. There was something unworldly about Hawthorne and his tales; yet the men and women he avoided were seizing upon his stories and paying him with worldly money. Margaret was a genius, uttering a jargon which few could understand; yet now she was traveling through the West, where eager little groups were clustering to hear her speak it. These were Channing's friends; he belonged to them; they admired his own talents. His little book had perhaps justified his membership. It was good to be a part of this brave new world.

It was good also to enjoy at home the atmosphere conducive to poetic creation. Occasionally he was obliged to make tea or to wash dishes, as Ellen's health was still uncertain; usually, however, his physical labors were confined to the woodpile and the garden, which better befitted his profession of poet. Sometimes he chopped wood for Emerson, who paid him fifty cents per cord.[44] Ellen too was adding to their income; by July she was taking pupils at the Red Lodge.[45] (Emerson paid tuition for his daughter Ellen at one dollar a month.) [46] In August they gaily invited young Richard Fuller to join them in a week's tour of the Berkshires.[47] Life was rich and varied.

Caroline Sturgis visited Emerson for several days in late August, and passed a night with the Channings.[48] For Caroline, this was a test of fortitude. She had been in love with love in those dreamy days on the Artichoke, and had identified love with Ellery. When the tone of his letters cooled perceptibly, and when the news of his engagement chilled her heart, it was almost more than she could bear. She had known that their tender friendship had been built of shining mist—but she had entertained too much faith in its foundations.[49] And such a choice as he had made! She was sure that Ellen—for whom she felt true affection—was no match for Ellery in nobility.[50] Caroline regretted that so many of her friends were taking unequal partners; it seemed more like adoption than marriage.[51]

She immersed herself in *weltschmerz*. There was comfort in the glooms and the lightning flashes of *Festus*.[52] She read Wordsworth and the other English Romantics. She wrote to Margaret: "I would gladly see the earth open to receive me into her bosom, that I might roll round and round with her and be at rest." [53]

Now, in August, she was ready to meet Channing face to face.

She found him happily married, and there is no evidence that her visit was in any way disruptive. Soon he and she resumed correspondence. "Occasionally Ellery and I fire pistols at each other," she said to Emerson.[54] But it was a friendly warfare, waged at moderate temperatures.

Although the day was still golden, there was trouble just below the horizon. A volume of Channing's *Poems* had fallen into the hands of the rising young critic Edgar Allan Poe, who was no friend of New Englanders and Transcendentalists. Upon William Ellery Channing Jr., this unknown versifier with the distinguished name, Poe let loose a barrage of jagged wit in a review which one scholar has declared to be "perhaps the most contemptuous he ever wrote." [55] The essay appeared in *Graham's Magazine* for August, 1843. Of the poems, Poe said: "They are full of all kinds of mistakes, of which the most important is that of their having been written at all. They are not precisely English—nor will we insult a great nation by calling them Kickapoo; perhaps they are Channingese." [56] After twitting the poet on his celebrated name, Poe proceeded to make merry over that capriciousness of rhyme and meter that even Emerson, Channing's chief apologist, was unable to condone. The essay was a masterpiece of devastation.

Channing's poetry was vulnerable at many points, and Poe exploited them all: the clumsy inversions, the unnatural shifting of accent, the frequent fuzziness of idea, the bravado and bombast as Channing stated his relations with the Universal Spirit. These are very real faults, and most of them are illustrated in the final stanza of "A Poet's Hope":

I am not earth-born, though I here delay;
   Hope's child, I summon infiniter powers,
And laugh to see the mild and sunny day
   Smile on the shrunk and thin autumnal hours.
I laugh, for Hope hath happy place with me:
   If my bark sinks, 'tis to another sea.[57]

In this stanza Poe pounced on the second line, ridiculing the pronunciation of *infiniter,* in which the stress is forced onto *nit,* and noting that *infinite* scarcely admits degrees of comparison. (Emily Dickinson, in her love poem " 'Twas a Long Parting," has the iambic line "Born infiniter now." Poe would not have liked Emily, either.) He spared comment on the last line of the poem, which was already a favorite among the Transcendentalists.

A critic less captious than Poe, however, would have discovered felicitous phrases throughout the volume, and occasionally images well conceived and sustained. Such a critic might have praised a little stanza called "Moonlight." Poe offers "a copy of the volume, if anyone will tell us what the lines are all about," but the sympathetic reader, even in 1843, could hardly have thought the poem cryptic. This is it:

He came and waved a little silver wand,
   He dropped the veil that hid a statue fair,
He drew a circle with that pearly hand,
   His grace confin'd that beauty in the air,
Those limbs so gentle now at rest from flight,
Those quiet eyes now musing on the night.[58]

The poem offers melody, delicate imagery, and a consistent tone—qualities that Poe usually admired. In Channing's work he was unwilling or unable to distinguish them, ap-

Henry M. Channing

Ellery Channing late in life

Henry M. Channing

Dr. Walter Channing, Ellery's father

Harvard in 1833—"the Peirce view"

Harvard University Archives

Curzon's Mill and the Artichoke River. Etching by Menzo Von Esveldt

The Perkins mansion,
first home of the
Boston Athenaeum

Ellen Fuller Channing

The Sanborn-Hosmer house, Channing's last home.
Engraving by Lester Hornby

Mrs. Margaret Crane Fuller and family
Eugene   Mrs. Fuller
Arthur   Ellen   Richard

pearing fitfully as they did among the less happy verses of the volume.

Channing was habitually reticent on all matters that concerned him closely, but years afterwards he wrote:

> Well I remember the rambles I took . . . after the printing of a Rev of my poems, how I ranged far and near, and formed theories of Art, and read faithfully in Goethe. Days of cold heart, days of mental and social poverty.[59]

If we look to the October instalment of "The Youth of the Poet and Painter" for these theories, or for other late news of Channing's mental life, we shall find hints that he is coming to know himself with a degree of critical objectivity. He has Matthews Gray say of Edward Ashford:

> What the world generally calls a poet, I believe he will never be, that is, to carefully prepare a good many dull verses, print them on the whitest paper, with notes of introduction, and engage a favorable critic to make them a pretty review. Whether he publishes anything, I consider doubtful; but from the poem you showed me, I judge the production of verse is natural to him, and that by abundant encouragement from his friends, he may be led to write with more attention to critical rules, though for some years he will pay the least possible respect to measure and formal art. . . . I would do my best to inspire him with a belief in his powers, though I should make a very gradual approach to any formal criticism of what he may send.[60]

Before the publication of Poe's attack, Emerson had sent a notice of the poems to O'Sullivan, the editor of the *Democratic Review*. The comment was published in September, with revisions and interpolations by the editor. Emerson recognized the first page as his own, however; and on that first page is the statement that "the author need not owe any advantage to the eminent name he wears, but is ready to add, to the distinction which already encircles it, the fame of poetry." [61] Channing still had a champion.

He sorely needed one. His self-confidence was badly shaken.

With the fall months another enemy of contentment began to make little raids on the arcadian cottage. Until then, illness had figured but little in the Channing idyl. Through the summer of 1843 Ellen had often been tired, but most of the time had managed the housework, with enough energy left over to teach the neighbors' children. By autumn, however, she was pregnant; heavy work brought on pains in the back. It was necessary that she lie down frequently during the day, and call on her husband more often than formerly to perform chores heavy and light. He made the fires, set the table, brought in the wood, prepared breakfast and tea, put away the dishes. He did his part, and tried to be cheerful at it, making weak jokes about the work and the worker. Still he disliked it. [62]

The farming season past, he concentrated outdoors on woodchopping, which he rather enjoyed.* The evenings still brought their calm for literary activity [63]—for scribbling the prose and poetry which he could send to *The Dial* with assurance, to the other magazines with hope.

So autumn congealed into winter, and winter melted into spring; and even the burden of housework and Ellen's growing weariness failed to interrupt the bucolic romance. When Channing's sister Mary became engaged to her second cousin Thomas Wentworth Higginson, Ellery was able to write her in this way about his own domestic life:

Marriage has proved to me a source of indescribable happiness; it has made life sweet, given me a wider faith in God,

---

* On Feb. 6, 1844, Emerson paid Channing $5 for chopping ten cords; on Apr. 15 he paid for fifteen cords. (Emerson, MS Account Books, Houghton)

and in man, led me to feel my connection with others,—but it is true, I have married a woman, everyway adapted to my character, to my views, my interests, my wishes, and my hopes. . . . There is no greater mistake, than to suppose, marriage grows tiresome after a while, and that the days of one's engagement only are sweet. It is my experience that each day of married life adds a new charm to the relation, deepens the faith of the husband and of the wife in each other, fortifies them against trial, suffering and misfortune, and increases, instead of diminishing their love. It is so in my own case, and I trust will prove so in yours.[64]

Twelve months after their arrival in Concord, the Channings moved to Lexington Road. For the same rental as that for the Red Lodge, they now enjoyed the advantages of a larger house on a more traveled highway. Again Channing faced the challenge of a garden.[65] But in latching the door of the Red Lodge for the last time, they ended a chapter which would remain dreamlike in the memory.*

* In the summer of 1852, as Channing walked near the red farm-house, he jotted in his notebook: "There is a house in which I spent one of the most happy years of my life." (Journal, Aug. 2, 1852)

The Wanderer

(1844–1847)

Margaret Fuller Channing was born on May 2, 1844; and, as any father to any neighbor, Channing reported her weight —seven pounds—to Hawthorne on their next fishing excursion.[1] But pride of fatherhood did not make up for the new annoyances. Immediately Channing was at odds with the nurse, Miss Prescott. Hawthorne, whose wife was away, thought briefly of inviting Channing to visit at the Manse, but concluded that the guest would wrangle with him too. "What a gump," Hawthorne wrote to Sophia. ". . . He should have been whipt often and soundly in his boyhood."[2]

Channing escaped to New Hampshire, and remained in voluntary exile until Miss Prescott had departed. In his absence, Ellen wrote to Margaret: "I have had some fine letters White Mountain wholly in their contents. . . . He wants to get back—but I fear to have him the baby cries so very much."[3]

Mrs. Fuller was at Ellen's side sharing the household duties; also a young girl who came in for two hours a day. But the baby was wakeful and demanding; and her mother was exhausted by these new responsibilities.

On Channing's return, he agreed that help was required. He himself wrote Margaret, bidding her to find a housemaid. Without one, he said, the housework would devolve upon him, "and I am a cipher." After reporting Ellen's fatigue and her immediate needs, he said:

If a woman of experience, somewhere between 30 and 40 years, I should suppose, could be found, willing to live in the *simplest* manner, to work constantly, for $1.50 per week, to do the housework and help Ellen take care of the child, we should feel only the more indebted to our friends than before.[4]

No such woman appeared. For a portion of the summer Channing eased the strain by joining Thoreau on a walking trip in the Berkshires and Catskills.[5]

It was doubtless Margaret who engineered a scheme which would reduce the need for a housemaid. After the Concord family had "stumbled along" through the summer months (the expression is Margaret's),[6] Channing accepted an invitation from Horace Greeley to join the staff of the New York *Tribune,* where his sister-in-law was about to take up her own duties. Characteristically, he approached the job by a devious route. In mid-November, while Ellen was packing for a winter in Boston at Dr. Channing's, her husband journeyed to Fishkill Landing, on the Hudson. Margaret was vacationing there with Caroline Sturgis, seeking refreshment of spirit before reporting to the *Tribune;* and Channing passed three days with them. One day they took a long excursion into the Catskills, where he and Thoreau a few months before had baked in the summer sunshine.[7] This brief autumn visit concluded, Channing moved down the river and went to work.

He entered the *Tribune* office on Nassau Street without any clear knowledge of either his duties or his wages; and no record of either remains. On his arrival Channing found

Greeley ill and about to vacate the editorial office for an indefinite period. "He threw to Channing some broadest general directions, and left him to make his own work,— the one thing he could not do," Emerson reported on December 3. "He has met with much vexation, I infer, and desponds a good deal, though resolved to stay, if he can." [8]

He seems to have shunned all society. To be sure, he roomed successively with Emerson's bachelor friends Giles Waldo and William Tappan,[9] but declined the cordial invitations of William Emerson, who tried to lure him to Staten Island.[10] Though his office colleagues found him amusing and lively, his heart was in Massachusetts. He wrote homesick poems, "To My Wife" and "The City," [11] and asked Richard Fuller, who moved to Cambridge in February to study law, whether he would visit Ellen in Boston several times each week, because "there are a hundred little things always to be done." [12]

Poems were a daily feature of the *Tribune*, and Channing may have written most of them, though they were signed by a variety of names. "To My Wife," which we know to be his, was ascribed to "Werner, New Bedford." None of Channing's contributions carried his own name. Margaret regularly did the book reviews, signing each with an asterisk; but the comment on her own book, *Woman in the Nineteenth Century*, bore the signature "C."

On marriage [said C] the author discourses, though briefly, with the solemn tone befitting the sacredness of the subject. . . . Marriage is truly a sacrament. The hope of the world is in the prevalence of the highest view in regard to the act of becoming parents. Only pure parents can aid through their children to elevate the race. Only children born of earnest love can be fitted to enrich humanity with beautiful and benign lives.[13]

Margaret had no opportunity while on the *Tribune* to review the poetry of her brother-in-law. She did, however, produce a column on Poe, in which she praised "To Helen," but added a paragraph which may have been a sop to Channing's feelings:

A person of fine perceptions, and unacquainted with the writings of Mr. Poe, observed, on looking at this head of him, that the lower part of the face is that of the critic, cold, hard, and self-sufficient; while the upper part, especially the brows, expresses great feeling; and tenderness of feeling. We wish the "Psyche" had taken him far enough in that "Nicean bark," to give the expression of the upper part of the face a larger preponderance than we find in his reviews of the poets.[14]

On March 5 Channing wrote to Thoreau, then in Concord:

I see nothing for you in this earth but that field which I once christened "Briars"; go out upon that, build yourself a hut, and there begin the grand process of devouring yourself alive. . . . Eat yourself up; you will eat nobody else, nor anything else. Concord is just as good a place as any other. . . . I saw Teufelsdrockh a few days since. . . . Says he, "That fellow Thoreau might be something, if he would only take a journey through the Everlasting No. . . . He is too dry, too confused, too chalky, too concrete." *

Channing himself had decided to return to the soil; perhaps he was for this reason the more ready to urge the move upon his friend. As early as February he and Ellen had resolved to buy a farm, and she had begun the search. ("I trust it may be a little one," said Margaret.) [15] It is understandable that with the first breath of spring Channing abandoned his desk at the *Tribune* office and sped to Concord, where he quartered with the Emersons.[16]

* This reference to *Sartor Resartus* and that at the close of this chapter demonstrate the currency of Carlyle's literary coinages. Emerson, it will be recalled, had brought about the original publication of *Sartor*. (W. E. C. to Thoreau, Mar. 5, 1845; Harding)

For a month he explored, debated, decided, reconsidered. Then it was settled.[17] On April 30 Emerson was able to report to Anna Ward a pair of events, not unrelated: "Ellery has just bought his land. Mr. Thoreau is building himself a solitary house by Walden Pond." [18]

Channing's acreage was the Brown farm, on the slope of Punkawtasset Hill, more than a mile from the village as one traveled out the Carlisle road. For twenty acres of woodland and tillage land Channing paid $600. There was neither house nor barn.[19] Channing arranged immediately for the building of a cottage which should be ready before the end of summer.

In early September they moved in.[20] Wentworth Higginson, one of the first to inspect the Channing farm, wrote to his mother:

Last Monday I went to Concord on a spree to a convention. . . . I went out to Ellery's, it is a beautiful situation and they have a nice little house built for $800! . . . Ellery was as kind and polite to me as possible, urged me to come up and stay sometime! Ellen and I are always friends and Greta * was thoroughly hospitable. The poet looked more seedy than I have words to express—his shoes bright orange, but this is nothing new, Mary says.[21]

Caroline Sturgis also offered a glimpse of the Channings at home, in a letter to Margaret on Thanksgiving Day:

I passed one afternoon this week at Ellen's—Ellery was sick and sepulchral, but civil; Ellen lonely as she always is now—at home at least, and I believe she is gentle everywhere. Greta is very cunning—she has every now and then freaks of fun, without any apparent cause, just as Ellery has. . . . I never saw a prettier external life, but pearls are hollow.[22]

* Greta was the earlier of Margaret Channing's pet names. She was also called Marnie.

In February Channing issued a new proposal, causing an exchange of indignant letters among the Fullers.[23] The resentment of his in-laws was tempered, however, by one inescapable fact—his preposterous plan had Ellen's full support.

He had resolved to go abroad. As a poet, he required stimulation. Having drawn from America what she could offer, he must turn to Europe, and study her art at first hand. He invited George W. Curtis and George Bradford to pass a year with him in Italy.[24] Such a period, he felt, should give him what he needed. Money would be essential, of course; he got off to Margaret an eager letter requesting her to ask Mr. Greeley to take him on as a foreign correspondent, with $100 to be paid in advance.[25] He wrote George Ticknor and the Honorable Caleb Cushing, both old friends of his father, asking them for contributions. Ticknor refused, but Cushing sent the $100 requested. Caroline Sturgis, then living with the Emersons, pledged $75. Emerson offered a like amount,* and wrote to Ward for $50. This made $300—the sum which Channing considered adequate for a year of life abroad, including passage money. If necessary, he could travel in the steerage for $25. Emerson wondered how Channing had arrived at this estimate of a year's expenses, but thought it advisable to limit the poet's resources; for Ellen Channing had said of her husband, "If he has money, he only spends it in idlest indulgences." [26]

It is unlikely that Margaret mentioned the project to Greeley; but with $300 assured, Channing was unconcerned. Nor was he deterred by the fact that Curtis and Bradford declined their invitations.

What aroused the Fullers most was not the presumptuous

* On Feb. 13, 1846, Emerson paid Channing $25 for "literary work." Presumably this was payment for labor already performed and was unrelated to the European venture. The gift of $75 was made on Feb. 25. (Emerson, MS Account Books)

fund-raising, but the timing of the adventure, which would remove him from the country during Ellen's second confinement. Margaret exclaimed over "the unnatural selfishness of a man who, having brought a woman into this situation of suffering peril and care, proposes to leave her without even knowing whether she lives or dies under it." [27] Caroline wrote to Margaret: "I suppose you think his scheme of going abroad a wild and even ruthless one, but if you could talk to Ellen about it you would agree with her, that he had better go. He cannot keep himself peaceable in the house, even now, when she has a girl, and it will be worse in the summer." [28] Channing himself reminded Margaret that he was "a bugbear in the house . . . during the first year of a child's life." [29] One recalls Ellen's dread of his return from the White Mountains, two years before.

One morning near the beginning of March, Channing trundled his luggage down the Carlisle road toward the Concord railroad station. As he passed the "Bullet-Hole House," which had been punctured in the skirmish of '75, Judge Keyes called out:

"Good morning, Mr. Channing. Where are you going?"

"To Rome," was the reply. The neighbors remembered this laconic answer, as an example of eccentricity.[30]

In some rather bad verses written later, Channing described his mood at this time. He was addressing Rome:

> I sought thee not a traveller vain,
> My heart was neither glad nor gay,
> My life had proved a life of pain,
> The flowers I love had bent away.
>
> Few friendly voices cheered me on
> Few dear caresses went with me,
> Alone I loved thee. . . .[31]

About the trip itself we know little except for its brevity. He sailed from New York on March 3, 1846, on the packet ship *Nebraska*, bound for Marseilles, Genoa, Leghorn, and Civita Vecchia.[32] He lay over at the ports of call, and presumably saw as much as he could. He spent sixteen days in the Eternal City, absorbing and recording.[33] Then he embarked once more on the *Nebraska*, reaching New York four months after he had left it.[34] On Independence Day he was back in Concord, making the acquaintance of a new daughter, Caroline Sturgis Channing.

Emerson reported Channing's return in a letter to the other Caroline. "He is very well, and has had a gratifying visit, and says that his journal is original, at least, and reads well; proposes that he will write it off, and be ready to print." [35] Another volume, however, was to precede the *Conversations in Rome*, thanks to Channing's considerate friend. When on October 21, 1846, Emerson contracted with James Munroe and Company for the publication of his own poems, he attached a rider providing for a new volume of Channing's verses on similar terms. In both cases the authors would pay the cost of manufacture, and the publisher would return 70 percent of the retail price on each copy sold.[36] Whether Channing covered the publication of his own book out of his meager income is not on record. Emerson received (and presumably paid for) at least seven copies of Channing's book when the little volume, dated 1847, appeared in late December of 1846.[37] He sent one of them to Longfellow, calling his attention to four particular poems, and remarking that the bookseller wanted *someone* to give the book a couple of friendly lines in the Boston *Courier*. Longfellow did not take the hint; he wrote a cordial letter of thanks, in which a few lines of faint praise of Channing's poems were sandwiched between his enthusiastic commendations of Emerson's.[38]

On January 1 the New York *Tribune* took notice of the book in a terse paragraph of generalizations. Channing's volume had "much poetry . . . some bad verse . . . poet's fire . . . poet's waywardness . . . merits . . . faults." Also in January the *Harbinger* commented on the Emerson and Channing volumes, along with one by William Wetmore Story. The reviewer found neither of the younger poets so "electrifying" as Emerson, but both more "human." He mentioned Channing's "difficulty in rhythm, and in the distribution of words in sentences," but praised the "wildflowers . . . still fresh with dew," and the "sturdy planting of both feet on the common earth." [39]

In the following weeks the two volumes were reviewed together on two other occasions: by C. A. Bartol in the *Christian Examiner* for March, 1847,[40] and by Francis Bowen in the *North American Review* for April. Bartol saw virtues in both poets; Bowen, whose journal was the more influential, tossed the poems of Emerson and Channing into the same basket as those of seven lesser poets, and showered all with sarcasm. "It passeth human patience," said Bowen, "to see one of these Noodles get down on his knees before a pigweed, and remain there mute with admiration, or standing open-mouthed after a bumblebee, and calling it a 'yellow-breeched philosopher.' If their disorder had not passed the use of medicine, we would counsel them to go and study Cowper's *Task*, and learn to be ashamed of their mystic ravings and transcendental silliness." [41]

Here, as elsewhere, Channing's verse offers the unfriendly critic a generous store of halting lines and doubtful usages. But the anthologist, concerned with the poet's best work, will find in the 1847 volume considerable stretches of quotable poetry. For example, here are the first ten lines of "The Lonely Road."

No track had worn the lone deserted road
Save where the fox had leapt from wall to wall;
There were the swelling, glittering piles of snow,
Up even with the walls, and save the crow
Who lately had been picking barberries,
No other signs of life beyond ourselves.
We strayed along, beneath our feet the lane
Creaked at each pace, and soon we stood content
Where the old cellar of the house had been
Out of which now a fruit-tree wags its top.

The meter is inconspicuous; the poet meets the demands of the blank verse pattern without sacrificing the illusion of natural speech. The images are sharp, and the sights and sounds are from direct experience rather than by way of books.

Of special interest is "Hymn of the Earth," which spoke in regular measures and vivid metaphor to an age that liked to personify the elements and to sense the flow of spirit through all Creation. In the first stanza, Earth says:

I rest forever on my way
　Rolling around the happy sun;
My children love the sunny day,
　But noon and night to me are one.

This last line reminds one of "Shadow and sunlight are the same" in Emerson's "Brahma," which was not to be published for ten years. There are, in these parallel verses, similarities of meter, alliteration, and meaning which suggest that "Hymn of the Earth" was one element in that amalgam out of which a much greater poem, "Brahma," was created. There can be no doubt about Emerson's familiarity with all the lines of this Channing volume which he had sponsored. But such borrowing, by a poet's unconscious alchemy, evades all proof. As with the relationship between Channing's "Spider" and Emerson's "Humble-bee," all we can be sure of is that we have an interesting coincidence which apparently went unnoticed by the poets themselves.

Conversations in Rome, between an Artist, a Catholic, and a Critic appeared late in June of 1847. Months before, Hawthorne had written his old friend Evert Duyckinck, the editor and critic, about the *Conversations,* asking for his help in finding a publisher; and then had sent him the manuscript. It may have been Duyckinck who placed it with Crosby and Nichols of Boston.

The critics who greeted the volume were friendly but somewhat patronizing. "A pleasant little memorial of a trip to Rome" opened the review in the *Literary World* of New York, which thereupon gave its main attention to the format, the dedication to Caleb Cushing, and the author's name. "It mars one's associations to meet with another William Ellery Channing in print, after the name has become hallowed." The reviewer gave two sentences to the contents, noting their Emersonian qualities.[42] The *Tribune* was more direct, calling the sketches readable and instructive, but deploring occasional obscurities, and preferring the prose to the verse.[43]

Emerson wrote to George Bradford, "Have you seen Ellery's book on Italy? Those who wish for his popularity, will conceive new hopes now that he has written so readable a book, and one that approaches so near to his style of conversation."[44]

Readable it is, even today, though it is hard to believe that Channing ever talked like his three sightseers. Mainly they utter monologues, some of them a page or more in length, before they yield the floor. The Artist, who has the most to say, often rhapsodizes, but attempts to discriminate also. For example:

In Domenichino, I perceive a thoughtful mind, wrestling with the difficulties of expression. He proclaims himself unvanquished, yet does not, like Raphael, glide with winged feet over the obstacles which embarrass the course of daring genius. Raphael parts the waves of expression, like a swift, sharp vessel under easy sail, that moves with immense rapidity, while Domenichino, with all his canvas spread, labors in the sea, through which he does at length triumphantly pass. In the picture of "Diana with her Nymphs," he seems to have for once forgotten himself, and, like a brilliant dream of youth, this charming and graceful band of beautiful women, a conception as chaste as it is fresh and inspiring, idealizes my former view of this great master's works.[45]

The Artist, in most of his lines, seems to be Channing dressed in a smock. Ostensibly, however, the author is the Catholic; and the speeches labeled "Myself" defend or explain sympathetically the positions of the Church. While the Artist and the Catholic differ occasionally on the claims of art and religion, they are generally respectful of both—unlike the Critic, a captious commentator with a sneer in every line. This, too, was a part that Channing could play with ease. Ellery the romantic had always alternated with Ellery the fun-poker, and the structure of *Conversations* allowed the author to say yes and no almost in the same breath.

In matter and phrasing the book is suggestive now and then of Browning's dramatic monologues. *The Bishop Orders His Tomb* had been published in 1845, and Channing may have been echoing the dying churchman in his lines of blank verse:

> We rapidly rush downward to our graves,
> Time, and the storms, and winters are upon us. . . .[46]

He may have reflected that convulsive grasping at immortality in the comment of the Artist:

. . . some Pope causes an admirable picture, the ornaments of an altar, or fine marbles for the walls, to be contributed, in order that he may cause to be graved there his name in stone. A great man dies, and is buried at the foot of the shady columns. . . .[47]

Another passage also reminds us of Browning—this time of "Fra Lippo Lippi," published eight years later. The theme of Browning's monologue comes doubtless from the biographical sketch in Vasari's *Lives of the Painters*. There is no evidence that the poet had read Channing's *Conversations*. But Channing, treating the same theme, has what Vasari lacks—the element that makes the monologue dramatic. Channing, speaking of Raphael, imagined the artist at war with himself, and said:

. . . I have no doubt that he was glad to escape from painting saints, when he could, and preferred his Fornarina before the Pope and all the Cardinals.[48]

Browning made the artist's tension memorable in the lines where Fra Lippo Lippi is drawn to the window by the Carnival below:

> And I've been three weeks shut within my mew
> A-painting for the great man, saints and saints
> And saints again. I could not paint all night.

Conversations in Rome has, throughout, the raw material of drama.

This productive year of 1847 brought Channing new recognition when for the first time he was anthologized. In *The Sybil, or New Oracles from the Poets,* editor Caroline Gilman quoted seven of his poems—but only one of Emerson's and none of Poe's.*

Yet success measurable in dollars still eluded Channing,† and he appears at this period to have lost any expectation of it. But instead of railing against the reading public for its obtuseness, he looked within himself and acknowledged a limitation. This writer who, as a schoolboy, had inhaled nitrous oxide and leaped like a grasshopper, now sampled a newer anaesthetic—ether—and read his fate in the pounding images. When and why he sniffed the gas is unknown; he may have been invited to sample it by his father, who was using it in childbirth cases.‡ Whatever the occasion, it produced fantasies that were instructive. On this event Emerson made a journal entry in July, 1847:

W.E.C. describes the effect of sulphuric ether as a whole railroad train driving all the time thro' his brain: he is fast arriving at the jumping off place: that which he has been searching for in all his life, he is now just on the edge of finding; but, over all this power on the tiptop, is perched still a residuum of the old state, the old limitation, and he learns that it can in no wise be got rid of; so that sulphuric ether "shows him the ring of necessity." Brandy, opium, nitrous oxide gas, sulphuric ether, hell-fire itself, cannot get rid of this limp band, O Asa! [49]

* Mrs. Gilman (1794–1888) was widely known in her lifetime for her own prose and poetry on nature and the "domestic affections."

† No figures are available on the income from these Channing volumes. Their failure is to be inferred from the lack of any evidence to the contrary. Channing and his family continued to lament his want of success with the public; had there been the slightest glow of hope on the horizon, it would have been reflected in the voluminous Fuller correspondence and in Emerson's journal.

‡ The first use of ether as an anaesthetic in dentistry was on Sept. 30, 1846, when Dr. W. G. T. Morton tried it out on one of his patients. Its first use in surgery was in Morton's famous demonstration at the Massachusetts General Hospital on Oct. 14, 1846.

In *Sartor Resartus*, which Channing was reflecting here, Teufelsdrockh is encircled from his childhood by a ring of Necessity, which grows as he ages, and almost roofs him over, shutting out the light. So is every man surrounded; "happy he for whom a kind heavenly Sun brightens it into a ring of Duty, and plays round it with beautiful prismatic diffractions." [50] To Carlyle, salvation lay in the recognition of one's limitations, coming to terms with them,—and going to work. "O thou that pinest in the imprisonment of the Actual, and criest bitterly to the gods for a kingdom wherein to rule and create, know this of a truth: the thing thou seekest is already with thee, 'here or nowhere,' couldst thou only see!" [51]

But with all the help of Teufelsdrockh and sulphuric ether, Channing could not break the bars of his prison. For him no heavenly sun transformed the ring from Necessity to Duty.

Near Home
(1847–1852)

For seven years after his return from Italy, Channing lived unobtrusively in Concord with Ellen and their increasing brood of children. In the cottage on Punkawtasset Hill until 1849, then in a village house on Main Street opposite the Thoreaus, the Channings preserved the appearance of domestic tranquillity. Nor was this wholly an illusion. Ellen managed to feed and clothe her household on something like $400 a year, mainly contributed by Channing's father. She provided also a warmth of affection to supplement the simple diet and homemade dresses. Loving beauty, she taught her children to see it in their surroundings. A little girl who was served tea with the Channing children under the apple blossoms on Punkawtasset Hill would always remember Mrs. Channing's golden curls, which made her look like an angel, and Mrs. Channing's remark that she was having tea outdoors because she so loved the blossoms.[1] Channing, who also loved blossoms, found his satisfactions in his woodland walks and in conversation with his friends. Discouraged more and more by the "ring of Necessity," but fitfully buoyant, he could be a most agreeable companion; outside the family his dark humors injured nobody and were at times even entertaining. As the family grew larger and noisier, Channing reduced the tensions by spending less time under his own roof. Thus a *modus vivendi* was achieved that made life possible and sometimes even pleasant.

In certain respects Channing had never grown up. He was still the boy whose manservant had done the chores, leaving him free to row his little boat, or to seek peace in the hushed alcoves of the Athenaeum. In place of the manservant he now had a conscientious wife, often assisted by her mother or an Irish maid. He had a rowboat, a continuing consolation. But he lacked the Athenaeum or any sanctuary to which he could regularly repair for study and for writing. For him the least satisfactory aspect of family life was the clamor and confusion. Even in the spacious Main Street house, the sounds penetrated to the attic, where he tried to isolate himself. Sometimes he showed impatience. Yet the children suffered more from his neglect than from his abuse.

As for Ellen—the Concord neighbors knew that she was always tired and often sick. Few suspected how steadily she was being worn down by emotional conflict. She went about her cooking and cleaning, and held her tongue.

In 1841 Ellen had listened to an inner voice that demanded she marry Ellery Channing. The outer voices, which demanded otherwise, she had disregarded. The ecstasies of their first two years, in Cincinnati and at the Red Lodge, had confirmed in Ellen's mind the eternal rightness of her choice. The ecstasies passed, but the conviction persisted. Even that grinning poverty, which Channing had claimed he could answer with a smile, failed to shake her loyalty. The girl whom George Keats had found to be a bundle of whims and tantrums accepted the harsh facts of her married life with hardly a hint of resentment. Occasionally she complained about the heaviness of her limbs, or the lightness of her purse; almost never about the man who—had he been differently constructed—would have relieved her ills or prevented them entirely. During a dozen years of marriage no suggestion that her husband was inadequate crept into her most intimate letters to mother and brothers—except once, when she asked Richard, in 1851, about the law on the custody of children in case of a separation. Hers was a lonely task, she added,—to raise her children unassisted and often opposed.[2] That was all. The subject did not reappear in her letters until late in 1853.*

Ellen Channing was a blend of inherited traits and complex conditioning which cannot be completely analyzed. Yet there are clues to her loyalty and her reticence. There was the doctrine of self-reliance, or reliance on the divinity within, which, though no philosopher herself, she would have inclined to believe if only because Mr. Emerson and Margaret believed it. This doctrine had justified her impetuous act in 1841 and offered convenient support for whatever course she wished to follow. There was her father's insistence that his children "stick to their bargains"; this may have determined in part the decision she must have made again and again to see the contract honored to the end. If in desperate moments she was tempted to lament her marriage openly, she was probably restrained by family pride, by a sense of propriety, and by a subconscious reluctance to admit that James Perkins had, after all, been right. But such temptations came rarely, if ever. Most of the time she was convinced that God had married her to Ellery,

---

* As early as 1846 Richard wrote to Margaret: "I have given up Ellery; I think Ellen will be separated from [him] *in time, when it is more convenient than now;* though she says she is not prepared yet to wish it." I suspect that Ellen's remark was not volunteered, but was in answer to Richard's question. Richard's letter to Margaret is dated Feb. 16, 1846. (Houghton)

and that the pain and poverty she suffered were the in-scrutable workings of His will.

Mrs. Fuller, who visited the Concord household for weeks at a stretch, was less reticent than Ellen, but on the whole a friendly critic. We have seen how, after the shock of the marriage, she accepted her son-in-law cordially and could even praise him on occasion. In her letters from Concord to her other children, she often mentioned Channing's kind attentions. On the other hand, she spoke frequently of El-len's path of discipline, her loss of earthly blessedness, her beauty gained through self-sacrifice; and Mrs. Fuller did not gloss over the cause. "We may be more than reconciled when we see with angels' eyes into the design of her union with E," she said.[3] Her attitude toward Channing was one of com-passion rather than resentment. The man had just been built that way, and not much could be done about it.

At least she could use her hands to lighten Ellen's work; she tried to be in Concord at all periods of greatest stress. One of these was on and after April 13, 1849, when the third child, Walter, was born. For more than five weeks Ellen was confined with inflammation of the leg. "She shed many tears the day before I left," her mother wrote to Margaret. "Her anxiety is always for her little girls subjected as they must be to much that is painful for her to hear and not relieve." [4]

These painful sounds would have been heard with even greater frequency if Channing's friends had not welcomed his companionship. Outside the house, his humors were sel-dom ill; and when they were, his comrades took amusement from them.

Of Channing's Concord friendships, the earliest and the longest was with Emerson. "Incomparable" and "inexhaust-ible" were words used by the older poet to describe his elfin disciple. He knew that, if necessary, he could live with-out Channing; but he knew also that such a life would be

poorer for the omission.[5] He tried to phrase what it was that
Channing offered him; he concluded that the younger man,
like seven others whom he noted down, was not "impart-
able." [6] Surely Channing's talk had a quality not to be found
even in his writings, which were unworthy of the man.[7]
Emerson tried to preserve this quality on paper by jotting
in his journal Channing's random comments. Some of these
were preposterous overstatements:

What a climate. One day, they take the cover off the sun,
and all the Irishmen die of drinking cold water; and, the next
day, you are up to your knees in snow.[8]

The merit of Irving's *Life of Goldsmith* is that he has not
had the egotism to put in a single new sentence. . . . So Pope
had but one good line, and that he got from Dryden.[9]

Emerson liked, too, Channing's audacious metaphors. A
certain philosopher was "a rocket with two or three mill-
stones tied to it." [10] Channing questioned whether "S" had
not the "requisite number of stamens." [11] Even after a disappointing ride to Marlboro, when neither landscape nor Channing had come up to expectation, Emerson could still call
his friend a "perpetual holiday," although he implied that
it might be better to use him only on special occasions.[12]

Channing's comments were expended lavishly; some
dropped unheard, some pounced out in such a rapid series
that their meanings were lost, some were just too cryptic for
comprehension. The spontaneity delighted Emerson.

It was not alone the comments that made Channing a
satisfying comrade. Ellery would call his friend's attention
to new combinations of old materials: of shadow and sunlight on a hillside, of birch and pine reflected in a quiet
pool—effects in Nature's kaleidoscope that might otherwise
have been missed. He had a true artist's eye; Emerson responded to these vistas and panoramas that Channing

pointed out. Ironically, the eye could not lend its talents to the hand, for Emerson recalled that when Channing had painted a tree on a barrelhead, Mrs. Channing had not known what it was supposed to be. Yet his perceptions of form and color were acute and discriminating.[13]

There was no condescension in Emerson's friendship for Channing. Occasionally he was critical of the younger poet's negligent craftsmanship, but at the same time he recognized genius in the concepts and imagery to which Ellery gave imperfect expression. Protector of Channing and apologist for him, Emerson respected his eccentric personality and treated him as a peer. Men were variously constructed, Emerson seemed to say; this friend was burdened with certain impediments that interfered with worldly success. "This perseverance of his in writing and printing, read they or read they not," wrote Emerson to Margaret, "is an unexpected indemnity which Nature seems to have added to our poet for some small discontinuity which she suffered to occur somewhere in these fine wires."[14]

In September, 1848, Emerson noted in his journal that he and Channing walked together twice a week.[15] Judging from the frequency of references to Channing in Emerson's journals and letters, we may accept this as a rough measure of their association over many years. Even after Channing became Thoreau's close neighbor and the two younger men strengthened their own walking partnership, Emerson continued to be the frequent companion of both.

The removal to Main Street occurred in the spring of 1849.*

* Although the deed for the Main Street purchase was signed June 25, the Channings seem to have moved more than two months before. A letter from Mrs. Fuller to Margaret dated May 21 says: "They have left their pretty cottage and moved to the village." (Fuller papers, Houghton.) The same letter reports the birth of Walter on Apr. 13, and Ellen's subsequent illness of five weeks. Mrs. Fuller does not speak of the removal as having just occurred, or as having presented any problems because of Ellen's weakened

Emerson had advised Channing against giving up the Punkawtasset house, saying that if it were his he would hold
onto it as long as he could see. "Who buys Channing's house
buys a sunset," he wrote in the journal.[16] However, there
were sunsets elsewhere; and since Channing had never
farmed the land, his ownership of twenty acres was pure
luxury. For Ellen, who had suffered from loneliness on the
hill, the move promised at least some friendly contacts with
her neighbors to punctuate her days of endless housework.
So in place of his cottage, barn, and hillside, Channing now
became the owner of a substantial village house dating from
1767; and a single acre of land which reached back and
down to the shore of the Sudbury River. The two parlors
facing on Main Street were delicately paneled, with fine classical mouldings; but perhaps Channing was more attracted
by the convenience of tying his boat to his own willow
branch.[17]

The rowboat, useful though it was, must occasionally be
abandoned for the stagecoach or the railroad train. Even in
these seven years of tame existence near home, there were
several excursions, each one of a week or longer, to unfamiliar tramping grounds.

He visited Hawthorne in Salem for two weeks in October,
1847, while Sophia and her two children were out of town.
Hawthorne was then "Surveyor for the District of Salem and
Beverly and Inspector of the Revenue for the Port of Salem."
Among his duties was to go about the wharves testing the
strength of rum to be exported to Africa. He said to Channing,
"I am determined the niggers shall have as good liquor as
anyone gets from New England." [18]

The Hawthornes had moved in September to 14 Mall
Street, a house in which his mother and two sisters occupied

condition. I believe, therefore, that the Channings were already
settled in the Main Street house before Walter was born.

a separate apartment. From the back of the house Channing could see an old Gothic dwelling with five gables. To this ancient relic Hawthorne would later add two gables out of his imagination.[19] Each afternoon they would take an "immense" walk—immense by Hawthorne's standards; and after Channing had eaten like an anaconda, they would talk till midnight.[20] Hawthorne found the companionship pleasant, though two weeks of it seemed to him quite enough.[21]

Two of Channing's trips have been reported memorably by his fellow walker Henry Thoreau: the first of their visits to Cape Cod in October, 1849, and the Canadian expedition of 1850. But Channing did not require a partner on his travels. In May, 1852, he tramped the sands of the Cape by himself. Arriving in Provincetown on Tuesday the fourth, expecting to stay one night only, he lingered from day to day, scribbling verses, jotting down disjointed observations. "If you once get fairly into this land of packets, winds, tides, storms, and inactivities, it is quite beyond exact computation when you may get out again," he noted.[22]

The killdeer and the mayflowers claimed his attention; also all localisms of speech and manners. He was amused to hear a man called a masterpiece because he mastered his mother. He was impressed by the lack of gates, and the resultant practice of jumping over and crawling under fences. After six nights, he boarded a sailing vessel for Boston; here was more lingering, for once at sea they were becalmed, and Channing hung over the rail with a Portuguese sailor who described to him the customs of the Western Islands.

So he lived—at home and abroad—as if his daily life were waiting for a wind, and as if he had no responsibilities until the breeze began to blow.

These occasions when he went away from Concord provided a respite not only for the traveler but also for the family he had left behind. Sometimes they, too, would change the scene, as in October, 1849, during Channing's first Cape Cod journey, when Ellen and the children visited for three weeks in Rockport.[23] Sometimes they would stay at home; it was a vacation to be spared the complaints of their unhappy husband and father.

One of Channing's journeys, however, served to bring him closer to Ellen in love and sympathy. This followed upon the tragic events of July 19, 1850, when Margaret, then the Marchesa d'Ossoli, with her husband and little boy, drowned off Fire Island, sixty rods from the shore. Emerson immediately advanced $70 to Channing and Thoreau to take them to the scene of the disaster in order to recover whatever they might find of Margaret's in the jetsam washed upon the beach. For several days the two men combed the scraps of wreckage, examined packages and stray garments for identifying marks. Finally they came away with a precious trunk and several smaller articles.[24]

On receiving the calamitous news, Ellen had taken the children to her brother Arthur's house in Manchester, New Hampshire. Arthur was the pastor of the Unitarian Church, and Mother Fuller was currently a member of the family at the parsonage. Ellen knew that her mother would take comfort from the sympathetic presence of those who loved her most.[25] The house in Concord was still empty when Channing returned from New York. As often happened when Ellen and the family were out of sight and hearing, there swept over him an awareness that he was lonesome, that he was really very fond of his family. The mood would persist as long as there were no distractions to dispel it.

After a week or so, he wrote Ellen a long letter. In part it was a sincere attempt to bring consolation to a woman in her bereavement. In part it was just a love letter. It was simple, direct, honest. It speaks for the man he wanted to be and whom he thought himself to be:

Dear Ellen:

I was glad to get your letter, for I am a little anxious about you all, & a good deal lonely. It requires as much patience as I possess to remain here now, which is not saying much to be sure. . . .

Your consolation must be in yourself chiefly, yet I hope you will a little rely on me, for I value that, above all things else. For what do I live but for that, to be your complement in the days of sorrow. Perhaps I am too much bound up in your lot to be the wisest friend, yet I trust you will find me still in the right place.

I trust that our children may live and be your compensation. To me, who rarely or never suffer, being principled against it, they will I trust seem not ever unpleasing. Too near us, they sometimes disturb, yet how much should not parents rejoice to bear for their children. . . .

Did I not know, O dearest wife, that you must be blest in yourself, I might invoke the aid of some god to bless thee, but alas, my love has not even proved a blessing. My love to mother & the children.

Ever affectionately yours,

WEC [26]

September, 1851, brought Ellen a refreshing interruption in her daily round of cooking and cleaning. She had been ill all summer with a persistent cough; and when an invitation lay in her lap from her brother William, who offered to pay all travel expenses for a visit to his home in Cincinnati, she glimpsed a new hope of rest and recuperation.[27]

The children were provided for; other relatives saw to that. Caroline (or Itty, as the family called her) would accompany her mother. Greta would live with the Higginsons in the parsonage at Newburyport, where Wentworth occupied the Unitarian pulpit. Walter would go to Boston with his Grandfather Channing and Aunt Barbara.[28] Ellery, too, must be cared for. Mother Fuller, already in Concord, would remain a few days; after her departure there would still be Margaret, the Irish maid, to cook his meals and to sweep the mud from the front hall carpet.[29]

It was a part of William's plan that Eugene Fuller, then visiting in Boston, should escort his sister by the canal and river route. They left in mid-September—Ellen, Itty, Eugene, and Eugene's wife Eliza—stopped at Niagara for the women's first look at the Falls, then pushed on to Pittsburgh and the Ohio.[30]

Ellen rejoiced to see her sister-in-law Frances once again and to renew her Cincinnati acquaintances of ten years. She found William's children charming. But there were disappointments, too; the sojourn fell far short of its promise. Her health showed no improvement, and the hard dry cough threatened to keep her company all through the winter. Moreover, her brother's home depressed her; William thought too much of eating and sleeping, and thus evaded his share of responsibility. Frances was pregnant, and her nerves were taut. For Ellen, the rest cure she had glimpsed proved to be a mirage.[31]

She was to have returned to Concord right after Christmas, but was forced to wait longer, as the river was frozen tight. It was early January before a thaw loosened the ice and Ellen and Itty could start East.[32]

Meanwhile, Channing lingered most of the time in Concord, and thought himself lonely. He enjoyed his daily excursions with Thoreau, though one night Henry exhausted him by dropping in and talking until after ten. He spent some of each morning in composition. Sometimes he would amuse himself by teaching his little dog a trick, or by bringing him into the dining room for a lesson in manners.[33] He wrote long and affectionate letters to Ellen, giving local gossip and the details of his daily life.[34] When Greta wrote a loving message from Newburyport, he answered it tenderly.[35]

Late in October he traveled to Lenox, and visited the Hawthornes in the little red cottage that had been their home since May of 1850. Their landlord and nearest neighbor was William Tappan, Channing's roommate of *Tribune* days, now married to Caroline Sturgis. The Tappans had produced an engaging little sprite named Ellen to match the Channings' Caroline. Still other friends were nearby and shared in his entertainment—Sam and Anna Ward, whose new house overlooked the Stockbridge pond. And there were casual meetings with the Sedgwicks.

Of these several families Channing sent careful reports to Cincinnati, asking Ellen to burn the letters because his comments were so personal. At least one of his bulletins escaped this act of prudence. Channing's picture of Hawthorne and his household follows:

This place is given evidently to criticism. Hawthorne has perceived it. His ways not the ways of the world have attracted the attention of the people; his habit of not calling on people, & his having written some books have made him a lion. I do not know that he has felt this, but I think he has felt his lack of society. I do not know that he is absolutely discontented but he seems rather dry & out of spirits. He has lived here I know not exactly how long, a year & a half I believe, I suppose he has hardly seen a face beyond that of his wife and his children: a difficult life truly to live. One cannot explain why some people are miserable where others would be happy. I should I think I could survive such a life as the H's have led up here; still, I know not. He has surely taken a strange way to live not attaching himself to a single new person year after year having indeed scarcely any old acquaintances.

He thinks a good deal of coming to Concord, and possibly to buy a place. Such a plan I would not encourage. Assuredly he would get tired of his purchase, & then he would be obliged all his days to think of selling or again go to work moving. He always I believe finds fault with the people among whom he settles not at the best a good beginning to make. I should think Sophia could not realize his ideal at all. She is by no means prepossessing and has not added to her beauty by time. And she has none of the means whereby elegance & refinement may be shed over the humblest apartment. Her children brought up in the worst way for visitors, by themselves, never having been to school, have of course nothing but bad manners. They break in when not required, & are not in fact either handsome or attractive. But how could the parents help this. I have formed a very different opinion of the H's this visit from any I ever had before, and H. has greatly altered.[36]

As a description of Hawthorne and his situation, this has the value of a candid camera snapshot, and no more. Just as a freak of light or a momentary grimace will distort the features in a chance photograph, so Channing in his ten-day visit caught his host in a saturnine mood, and misread its meanings. Professor Randall Stewart has established the overall happiness of Hawthorne's family life, the expansion of his social circle (Stewart names sixteen of his Lenox visitors), and the improvement in his financial situation during those eighteen months in the Berkshires. But Hawthorne had recently grown restive; and his dissatisfaction with Lenox had been aggravated by a quarrel with the Tappans over the apples in the next orchard. His mood was a passing cloud, darkening the entire household for the period of Channing's visit. Three weeks later, the Hawthornes moved back to eastern Massachusetts.[37]

We have seen that Channing's affections bubbled up afresh whenever the petty irritations of his home life were removed. From his description of Sophia and the Hawthorne children, one may assume that he compared them silently with his own family, and that at the moment he preferred his own. Doubtless Ellen was similarly instructed by the unhappiness in Cincinnati. Thus they were fortified for another chapter of their life together.

Channing and Thoreau

(1851–1853)

Among the literary men of Concord, the closest comradeship was that of Channing and Thoreau. Except when one or the other was out of town, the two were for years almost daily companions. They walked and talked, botanized and geologized, nosed their boat into the pickerel weed of the Assabet, and scrambled over the hard crown of Monadnock until they knew intimately her rugged conformations. They scribbled sunsets and moonrises, robins and lichens into dozens of flimsy notebooks; and, perhaps the supreme test of friendship, they ventured into Concord's Lyceum to hear each other lecture.

Their friendship developed during Channing's stay at the Emersons' in the summer of 1842 and his subsequent visits to Concord through the fall and winter. It is not surprising that the men were drawn to each other. Both were born in 1817. Each echoed the other's enthusiasms and prejudices. Both wished to write, and to write boldly—not pretty verses in what Channing called the French fashion, but hard truths, such as a more muscular age might have chiseled in the primeval rock. Thoreau, critical of current educational methods and eager to free his style from Harvard rhetoric, had reason to look with respect on this other youth, who had defied family and tradition and abandoned Harvard in favor of a drafty grist mill. Three years before the beans were planted at Walden, Thoreau was ready to admire a man who had already lodged on the prairie. Both were students of nature—of Emerson's NOT ME; both were quick to notice correspondences in the NOT ME that surrounded them, and to crystallize the likenesses in metaphor and simile. Both enjoyed the friendship and the encouragement of Emerson. Thus they started in 1842 on common ground, which they were to tread together for twenty years.

We recall Lowell's lines in "A Fable for Critics" which paired the two so efficiently that later critics cannot decide which man stretched his short legs to walk in Emerson's footsteps, and which picked over Emerson's discarded apples.

All these years Channing and Thoreau were absorbed by the problem of living. Both were concerned with how to earn a livelihood without destroying the soul. Thoreau found a solution in simplifying his demands. "A man is rich in proportion to the number of things he can afford to let alone," he said in *Walden*. Giving up what he desired least in order to leave time and a little money for the essentials, Thoreau followed with rare consistency the pattern of life that he preached. Channing was never wholly converted to the doctrine of simplicity, though it was he who had suggested the Walden experiment in his letter to Henry in March of 1845. Wanting all things but wishing to pay next to nothing for them, Channing was frustrated and rebellious. But although his destination was less clear than Thoreau's, both men used the same paths. In their attacks upon the problem of livelihood and in the massing of their own defenses, they shared in a warfare with society; it was as comrades-in-arms that they made their sallies upon the Mill Dam and the Lyceum, and skirted the stone walls of Concord in scouting operations.

In the spring of 1845 Channing had returned to his wife and family on Punkawtasset Hill after his winter of editorial chores on Greeley's *Tribune*. From this time on, he and Thoreau pursued together three professions (as they called them): writing, observing, and lecturing. Furthermore, since the income accruing from these careers ranged downward from little to nothing, the men were forever laboring to justify their courses of life both to the world and to themselves. Both living on the defensive, they received from each other a moral support that even Emerson could not offer, for Emerson's career had been vindicated in terms of public reception. Social pressure cemented their partnership, though they would never have admitted it.

Let us look first at these parallel "professions," and then at the barricades behind which the rebels retired.

The first of these careers was writing for publication. I shall only touch upon it here; but certain similarities should be noted. Like Channing, Thoreau had found *The Dial* a ready outlet—at least after 1842, when Margaret Fuller surrendered the editorship to Emerson. But Thoreau had found, as had Channing, that Emerson's taste was not the taste of Massachusetts and the English-speaking world. Both men had knocked on the doors of the New York publishers, and had abandoned the metropolis after a few months. Channing had published three volumes of verse and one of prose by 1853, but these had met with no more success than Thoreau's *Week on the Concord and Merrimack Rivers*, of which the unsold copies towered in the author's attic.

The second vocation was observing. On November 9, 1851, Thoreau wrote in his journal: "In our walks C. takes out his notebook sometimes and tries to write as I do, but all in vain. He soon puts it up again, or contents himself with scrawling some sketch of the landscape."[1] And the following June, Emerson remarked: "Ellery is grown an accomplished Professor of the Art of Walking, and leads like an Indian. He likes the comic surprise of his botanic information which is so suddenly enlarged. Since he knew Thoreau, he carries a little pocket-book, in which he affects to write down the name of each new plant or the first day on which he finds the flower."[2]

This scribbling was the outward evidence of the new career. Unsuccessful in the roles of student, farmer, journalist, and poet, Channing was now becoming an "observer." He entered upon this vocation, as he had upon other ventures, with no little zest. He loved the woods and fields; he had an appreciative eye for white birches against the blackness of a swamp; he had an ear for the pipings of a meadowlark in a sunny valley. If birds and flowers and puffs of cloud could be caught up into a profession, Channing would turn them to that use. His heart, no less than his purse, cried out for steady employment; and here was promise that at least one of them would be rewarded.

It was no accident that Channing began now to label his favorite recreation a career. In this he was following Thoreau, whose journal shows at this time a major shift of attention from the classics to nature study. Since 1849, when Channing sold his Punkawtasset sunsets, he had been living on Main Street opposite the house which the Thoreaus occupied from 1850 on; naturally the association was closer than ever, and a change of vocational emphasis was contagious. For Thoreau this was no momentary whim; he was determined to become an expert in this science where he had for so long dabbled with delight.[3]

Thoreau's shift was duly echoed in his companion's note-book. For example, on April 17, 1853, Channing blamed a lack of observation for much bad writing. There was Hawthorne, he said, "shambling" through life, wrapped tightly in his cloak but even more tightly in himself, seeing nothing and hearing nothing except himself. Hawthorne had art, but "works of art should be works of nature too."[4] The artist, Channing concluded, is "he who, having more than ordinary susceptibility to impressions, and keenly alive in his perceptions of these, learns through culture to express them in forms of some kind or another."[5] This last vague phrase suggests how little respect he paid to the problem of form.

Speaking of the country life, Channing wrote: "If it is any better than ennui, it must be so, solely in its adoption as a business."[6] Hence he set to work recording his thoughts, feelings, and movements in the hope that the habit of observation would grow upon him;[7] that as he achieved proficiency in this craft, his *im*pression might be translated into *ex*pression. His one hope as a poet now lay in his ability to take a more thorough census of nature.

Channing took a humorous delight in displaying his technical knowledge because he knew, as well as Thoreau and Emerson, that he was no scientist. There was an incongruity in his acquaintance with technical terms, and his sense of humor recognized it. "I have bought a botany, of little use, no technical florist in me."[8] "I will never more than idly nibble on botany."[9] "I cannot [*sic*] not only not remember the names of the flowers from season to season but not even from day to day."[10] With such apologies the journal is sprinkled. It was in reference to such exact knowledge that he remarked to Thoreau: "I am universal; I have nothing to do with the particular and definite."[11] Yet when the mood was upon him, he went into minute detail. He read White's *Selborne*, which he found rather narrow; but White was writing for scientists, he realized.[12] Elsewhere, in order that he might call himself a naturalist, he whimsically twisted the word to fit his qualifications, saying: "A naturalist is one who does not know nature, i.e. scientifically."[13]

Channing had always been an acute observer in his haphazard way, and the journals draw sharp pictures as natural as the apple orchard that he crosses, and the pungent woodsmoke that his nostrils relish. Unhampered here by poetic archaisms, unbound by the demands of meter, to which he was wont to pay a nominal respect, and writing for no eyes but his own, Channing turned out glittering fragments.

His eye was keen to catch the shapes and shades of every season. He wrote in winter: "Most beautiful silvery appearance of frost on Button bushes & willows on the edge of the river . . . salmon-colored smokes . . . Shooting ice crystals at bottom of a ditch, like ivory blades to penknives radiating . . . dry oak-leaves rustling exactly imitate rain . . . Walden like a painting on glass . . . after sunset almost a black green if there is such a thing, & behind them the wonderful greenish or pearly light of after-sunset." [14]

The oral by-products of this new industry were picked up now and then by Thoreau, like chips in a basket. Henry's journal tells us that Channing compared the two of them in the spring to water insects coming out of their shells; called winter the Sabbath of the year; likened the knobs of ice that dropped from the twigs to lemon drops; noted that a distant flock of geese was "a black ribbon, almost perpendicular, waving in the air." [15]

Channing's faith in the value of his current profession was not unshakable. Perhaps the remarks of his companions diminished his zeal. He admitted at least twice that Emerson had laughed him out of taking notes on days when they walked together.[16] Perhaps also he realized that what he most needed for converting impression to expression was not a greater wealth of observation, with which his mind was already rich. On July 25, 1852, when he had been devoted to this new profession less than a year, he admitted: "Indeed one knows not if these forms of Diary be of any use at all.

At the best it is a great uncertainty." [17] In January of 1853 he wrote: "Today I have thought of noting Walden carefully on all sides. Yet nothing can be more barren than such notes. I see no hope of putting them into book form, nor that any mass could make a serious difference. They have their value as a little memory, & the habit of observation may thus be cultivated. This habit must be constantly aroused, as thoughts and feelings else overpower the observer." [18]

In April even the name of naturalist, however defined, seemed inappropriate. "I have lost in despair all hopes of attaining unto the degree of a naturalist," he wrote; "a natural, I still may pass for." [19]

Late in July Channing gave up his daily entries. He still walked and still observed, but the notes became occasional. He would continue to make jottings of many kinds; but taking notes on nature, which was to remain among his avocations, was no more mentioned even playfully as a profession.

The third career was lecturing, which Thoreau had pursued from 1838, when he gave his first dull reading before the Concord Lyceum. As a platform speaker, he had a limited appeal. He could be entertaining—and was, on rare occasions; but when his hearers were looking mainly for amusement, they were asking him for (as he put it) his "second best." One suspects that on the occasion when his audience laughed till they cried, he felt that he had been unfaithful to himself.[20] His lectures were usually too solidly sententious, giving the listeners no time to ponder. Only when he was emotionally aroused—as he would be later in defending an Anthony Burns or a John Brown—did he break loose into eloquence.

Channing began his lecture career on January 21, 1852, with the first of a series of three Wednesday evening addresses in Boston. His subject was "The Spirit of the Age."

It was a fine lecture, but spoken too rapidly, said one report.[21] Emerson had made calls on his friends to urge their attendance, but in spite of the loyalty of the Transcendental brethren the audience was small at all three programs. The venture had been poorly advertised, said Wentworth Higginson; a friend of his had traveled all the way from Salem to hear the third address, but could not find any notice of the meeting place and went to five halls without success. "I mention this," said Higginson, "because these incidents are valuable as showing us the necessity of studying the lower laws of conduct as well as the higher ones." [22] In the meantime, on January 29 Channing spoke at the Concord Lyceum on "Society." Mrs. Fuller, then visiting in Concord, went along to hear him, thankful that his energies had turned at last in a lucrative direction. She observed that many of the listeners had come expecting to hear Emerson, but she seemed to feel that they were not cheated. She found the lecture "rich in thought, brilliant, and witty." [23] "It was a bushel of nuts," wrote Thoreau in his journal that same night; and he went on to remark:

Perhaps the most original lecture I ever heard. Ever so unexpected, not to be foretold, and so sententious that you could not look at him and take his thought at the same time. You had to give your undivided attention to the thoughts, for you were not assisted by set phrases or modes of speech intervening. There was no sloping up or down to or from his points. It was all genius, no talent. It required more close attention, more abstraction from surrounding circumstances, than any lecture I have heard. For, well as I know C., he more than any man disappoints my expectation. When I see him in the desk, hear him, I cannot realize that I ever saw him before. He will be strange, unexpected, to his best acquaintance. I cannot associate the lecturer with the companion of my walks. It was from so original and peculiar a point of view, yet just to himself in the main, that I doubt if three in the audience apprehended a tithe that he said. It was so hard to hear that doubtless few made the exertion. A thick succession of mountain passes and no intermediate slopes and plains. Other lectures, even the best, in which so much space is given to elaborate development of a few ideas, seemed somewhat meagre in comparison. Yet it would be how much more glorious if talent were added to genius, if there were a just arrangement and development of the thoughts, and each step were not a leap, but he ran a space to take a yet higher leap.[24]

The next day Thoreau added:

Channing's lecture was full of wise, acute, and witty observations, yet most of the audience did not know but it was mere incoherent and reckless verbiage and nonsense. I lose my respect for people who do not know what is good and true. I know full well that readers and hearers, with the fewest exceptions, ask me for my second best.[25]

Channing followed these initial addresses with engagements in Providence, Worcester, and Fall River; possibly also in Greenfield. He also delivered three sermons. His mother-in-law wrote on March 9: "Ellery *preached* in Plymouth on Sunday. . . . It is said a new Church is to grow up in which a new order of righteousness is to grow up. This troubles F. T. Gray but not me for God is over all." [26]

The Reverend Frederick T. Gray of Boston need not have been alarmed—at least by Channing's efforts. One of the sermons, preached in Abington, was extempore and lacking in fluency. "It is most amusing to see people go to sleep while you are addressing them," Channing observed in his journal; "to see their eyes shut; to perceive the gradual extinction of their intellectual faculties. This must become quite an art with the pastor, to know the amount of sleep possible to his audience, & to hush them into absolute oblivion all around." [27]

Channing's lecture career ended with that spring of 1852. The rest was silence, except for some blurred plans that never were brought into focus. He begged Higginson to promote his lecturing, and announced that next winter his subject would be "Biography." Hardly knowing how to respond, Higginson asked a friend, "Can you encourage me by any better report of his new lecture or lectures?" [28] The answer is unknown, but Higginson arranged no bookings.

More sensitive than Thoreau to the indifference of his audience, Channing gave up the effort to further his own platform career. But again he and Thoreau had shared an experiment.

This parallelism of physical and mental life might well have encouraged a close acquaintance without making them comrades, but for one fact: that the world marked them both as failures. To understand the community of feeling that existed between Thoreau and Channing, we must take our perspective from those days before *Walden* was published, when both men were rated as irresponsible idlers, a trial to their families, and no credit to their town. The Concord of the early fifties never suspected that one of them would take his place among the prophets.

Probably the pressure was heavier on Thoreau. A village is most severe toward its own sons. He had made little of his opportunities, as far as one could see. His thrifty family had sacrificed to put him through college, but there was no sign that he had justified his education. John Thoreau had built up a profitable business which any true Yankee son should have been proud to carry on and expand; but not Henry. He helped his father scarcely two days a week. Once in his carelessness he had even set the woods ablaze, and ruined acres of timber. Of late years he had taken in a desultory income as surveyor. Admittedly he was a good surveyor, as he was an able pencilmaker and odd-job man.

Yet all he appeared to look for was a hand-to mouth existence.

If Henry's want of personal ambition was deplorable, his
apparent lack of responsibilitiy toward his family must have
seemed inexcusable to the gossips of the Mill Dam, the
downtown end of Main Street. It would require no wild
flight of imagination to reconstruct the substance of village
comment on this man who allowed his aging father to labor
in wood and graphite to support the household while Henry
stalked off daily into his carefree world of bird life and
botany. There is always man's work to be done about a
house—even a village house; a jobless man may keep busy
if he will. "Faith in God, faith in man, faith in work"—so
Lowell sums up the creed of the New England fathers. In
renouncing the third member of this trinity, Thoreau committed sacrilege.

To Concord, this was all of a piece with Thoreau's refusal
to pay the poll tax in 1846. Here was a man who recognized
no obligations to himself, to his family, to society at large.
The Concord farmer and the Concord shopkeeper could not
condone this trifling with divine law.

Channing, as an outlander from Boston, was, I should
suppose, less subject to these indirect and tacit reproaches.
There was no going business in graphite out in the Channing
woodshed, awaiting a little show of enterprise. Concord
knew, however, that Channings were traditionally leaders
of their professions, and that Ellery was somehow unworthy
of his illustrious name. Concord knew also that Channing's
family obligations were more importunate than Thoreau's,
that a man who adds to his household owes more toward
its upkeep than one whose family is merely inherited. Time
was to prove that Thoreau's position was the more tenable,
just as his powers to strike back at a critical society were
the greater. Channing could only dodge and duck; Thoreau
had a sharp weapon with which he was to put the world

on the defensive at last. But until the publication of *Walden* and to a degree thereafter, these two eccentrics were bound together by a common consciousness of the headshakings and whisperings behind their backs.

In 1867 Channing scrawled in a new folio journal:

I suppose the disinclination to meet wood-choppers comes from the idea, supposed to be attached, to the indolence attributed to the walker. He is looked on as a loafer, one who had better be employed at something else, a man out of work. Of course, it must look so. It excites envy, to see another loitering, when we are laboring, grinding our bones to get bread.[29]

This is an important comment. It explains why sometimes he and Thoreau, "when they went on an all-day walk, played a game to see how many farmhouses they could pass without being observed."[30] It explains also why they were most at ease in the company of such professional idlers as George Melvin, One-eyed Goodwin, and each other.

Certain of Channing's contributions to this companionship had their effect, one may suppose, on the personality and powers of Thoreau. Two have already been discussed: the moral support that helped to erect the cabin at Walden, and the sprightly perceptiveness that saw lemon drops in the snow and black ribbons waving in the sky. Channing brought something else, too: an extra dealing of Thoreau's own little vices and weaknesses—the tendency to exaggerate, the bushel-of-nuts style, and the boorishness. It must sometimes have seemed to Thoreau as if a caricature of himself were trudging at his side, a grotesque shadow with elongated features.

Thoreau wrote to Emerson of Channing's "characteristic exaggeration,"[31] and in his journal he confessed:

My companion tempts me to certain licenses of speech, i.e. to reckless and sweeping expressions which I am wont to regret that I have used. That is, I find that I have used more harsh, extravagant, and cynical expressions concerning mankind and individuals than I intended. I find it difficult to make to him a sufficiently moderate statement. I think it is because I have not his sympathy in my sober and constant view. He asks for a paradox, an eccentric statement, and too often I give it to him.[32]

Of himself he had written earlier, "I want things to be incredible,—too good to appear true." [33] Thus Thoreau recognized the disease as their common affliction; and the fact that he feared the perpetual contagion of Channing probably worked on the whole to moderate his considered observations on society.

So with the bushel-of-nuts style. That admirable epithet would apply quite as fitly to the staccato utterances of Emerson and Thoreau himself. Had Henry made no comments on Channing's incoherence, we might accept his silence as indicating the deafness of a provincial to the peculiar accents of his province. But Thoreau noted the lightning transitions. I repeat his remark: "How much more glorious . . . if there were a just arrangement and development of the thoughts, and each step were not a leap, but he ran a space to take a yet higher leap." [34] Although Professor Edward Tyrrell Channing would never have put it in this language, he may have given some such advice to young Thoreau in 1837.

There are no controls by which we can establish beyond argument or can measure the influence of Channing on Thoreau's style. Neither can we prove that Channing served as a brake on the extravagance of Thoreau's pronouncements. But I believe the evidence points that way.

It may be assumed that Thoreau's boorishness—his conscious avoidance of pretty manners—was similarly tempered by his friend's fits of rudeness. Channing could be insufferably loutish. It was as if he were haunted by a Godwinian fear that any social cooperation would threaten his individuality. Recounting a river journey, Channing wrote: "Met a boat with three men one of whom spoke but I did not reply. My 2/3 boat is not quite fast enough to speak a strange craft." [35] Thoreau deplored such conduct, as when he entered this incident in his journal:

Two young men who borrowed my boat the other day returned from the riverside through Channing's yard, quietly. It was almost the only way for them. But, as they passed out his gate, C. boorishly walked out his house behind them in his shirt-sleeves, and shut his gate behind them as if to shut them out. It was just that sort of behavior which, if he had met with it in Italy or in France, he would have complained of, whose meanness he would have condemned. [36]

It was a younger Thoreau who in 1841 had deliberately kept his seat while a lady stood. "No," he said to himself, "be true to your interests and sit; wait until you can be genuinely polite, if it be till doomsday, and lose not your chance everlastingly by a cowardly yielding to young etiquette." [37] Even then he had been troubled into two pages of self-justification.

The years seem to have socialized Thoreau to a degree; at least his rebellions in the 1850's showed more discrimination. To Channing, who was devoted to him, he could at times appear "dry as husks," one whose abstinence and chastities "have made him only doubly repulsive to his kind." [38] But Thoreau no longer valued bad manners for their own sake. I suspect that he recognized once again his own features in the shadow at his side.

Year of Escape

(1853)

Channing listened to a robin, caroling in the glow of an April sunset. Of all bird songs, this was his favorite. He scribbled in his notebook: "O that robin's evening song why is it so like old dreams of youth and of Heaven. Strange, familiar, homely and noble it goes before all description." [1]

Like the voice of Keats's nightingale, the evening song of the robin was eternal. Channing as a child had known it in Milton Hill, Northampton, Brookline, when all his dreams were promising fulfillment; it had played an obbligato to his reveries as he sat under the Harvard elms, or drifted down the Artichoke, or scratched at the Illinois prairie. The immortal note of promise in the robin's call must have struck Channing wryly in 1853, when the optimism of youth, with its many particular hopes, had changed to a chronic depression lightened only by intervals of escape to the woods. This depression, often bordering on despair, might be expected as a natural consequence of his failure in the three vocations which he shared with Thoreau. It is certainly indicated by his notebook comments, and confirmed by his behavior at home, where his relations with Ellen approached a crisis.

If the song of the robin suggested the girl with the heart-shaped face whom he had married in 1841, his thoughts were painful. He was sure that he had been the victim of illusions, as is ever the fate of the "man of fancy." "Things that are not will still look resolutely at him," he said; and "things" included persons. "Before the interview and for five minutes more, the angel lasts, and then all is over. Our saint is ugly, ungenial, coarse. The person was a fine hope, flattering and false." [2] In the place of his own delicate angel he had a sick wife, with three vexatious children and a fourth expected in June. Forever there was wood to be chopped, rubbish to be burned, grass to be mowed. The genius of poetry could find no lodging here. Only by tramping in the woods could Channing keep his sanity. "This walking is the recourse of lonely, literary men, whose thoughts would else become intolerable nuisances," he jotted in his notebook.

Although the annoyances of his domestic life were very specific, Channing generalized in his journal. "We have made great mistakes, such as we cannot repair, enduring, indispensable. Very well, they must be petted, coquetted with and enrolled. To leap, to kick, to make wry faces never touched the heart of the business in any manner." [3] Sometimes a situation got beyond the poet's endurance, and he damned his family up and down. Often he called his wife a fool, or an ass. To him there was provocation enough when he caught her teaching the children from a little book of scriptural history, or talking about an expensive education for the girls, who might better be schooled in housework.[4] But he made stabs at amiability: at petting his mistakes, coquetting with them and enrolling them.

In spite of dissatisfaction with his immediate society, Channing had no desire to withdraw from the human race.

To withdraw is to deny one's own nature, and one's nature will retaliate, he observed. Man's nature will cry out, "You may starve me and I will starve you." Channing believed that the more fortunate were protected from such folly by instinct, and he wrote a couple of pages about it, putting Emerson's doctrine of compensation to an odd use.

This instinct leads the young and beautiful girl, never to give up the party or the dance at the party or the most expensive dress for the party. She will not give up either the one or the other, yet all may look equally criminal and absurd. . . . And the plain one, the dowdy, gives them all up, and goes plain and dowdy. She attracts none, and none attract her. She admires none, and none admires her. . . . So each trifle that she omits—the elegantly stamped note-paper with her initials in the corner, the earrings, or the finger-ring, all cry out, you starve me and behold you are starved yourself. This absolute tit-for-tat, this ultimate bargain and illimitable compensation seems at once pitiful and terrible. We cannot bereave ourselves of a single advantage, no matter how much we may plume ourselves on duty and self-sacrifice but it rebounds and we are defrauded. [He cited Thoreau,] who has gone steadily along over the rough places and the thorns, in order to crucify and to kill out the human virtues, to render himself a Spartan. Each social faculty in which all others delight, he mortifies. Behold the victim of mortification. On him neither beauty nor goodness; you have him there, eminently chaste and abstinent, and at the same time dry as husks. . . . What is his compensation. Eternal solitude, and endless blundering, blunder after blunder."

This "repulsive" figure remained, at the same time, Channing's closest friend, his walking companion by choice, of whom he would later write a eulogistic biography. Now, in his notebook, he was dashing off another of his exercises, one of his watercolors in words, reflecting his current mood. He concluded that we must not deprive ourselves of what our nature craves—at least not wholly—but must "find that golden point in the balance, between thought and life." [5] Life, to him, must have included wife and children—those expensive but vital commodities that Thoreau had renounced. In contrast, Channing doubtless felt himself overendowed; for him, more thought was needed, rather than more life, if a balance was to be reached. But in principle the family was an institution to be cherished, however distracting to the man of thought.

Some of these notions were recorded, but most of his thinking vanished in a haze of reverie. His notebook jottings were mainly about such physical facts as landscape, birdsong, and thunder, for he was still the professional observer. Now and then he commented on his acquaintances, using the friends he most admired as standards of measurement. While visiting Ellen's Aunt Abi Crane in Canton, he tried to find in that tough and dry old lady some trace of Margaret's wonderful talent, but all he discovered was "considerable culture of a certain kind, limited." [6] Two days later, as he changed trains at Still River, he ran into a "refined and cultivated Depot-master fond of scenery and of retirement; in that a budding Thoreau." [7]

This pleasant encounter occurred as he set out for New York, on April 19, 1853, to ascertain whether the place was "of any practical value." [8] He may have hoped to renew his relations with the *Tribune*, but he made no record of any call at his old office. If the trip was merely an extension of his daily walk, it served its purpose: escape from annoyance and boredom.

He passed but one day in the city, doing a few errands, seeking out the house where Margaret had lived, and viewing the Egyptian gallery and the Dusseldorf pictures. He found the relics of the Pharaohs handsome, strange, numerous—and tiresome. New York itself he called wonderful, but "a mere mercantile phenomenon, in which there appears to be no particle of wit." [9]

The trip home was better—on the Fall River boat, along the smiling shores of Long Island, then by land following a devious route through Providence and central Massachusetts. At Worcester he listened to a tall young clergyman named Edward Everett Hale, "a genial, pleasing person, accomplished plainly eno." He climbed to the summit of Mount Wachusett, where the mayflowers grew profusely. The next night he spent in Princeton, at the foot of the mountain, watching a heavy rainfall with violet-colored lightning, and listening to the hylas sing through it all. In the morning he made note of a cane collection in the hotel barroom—seventeen different woods, all labeled: crabapple from Montrose, Iowa; white bay from Mobile, Alabama; holly from Charleston, South Carolina; apple from Princeton, Massachusetts. He listed all seventeen, and added a few words of praise for the little town: "Little or no society, no visiting done in this place. . . . A free people democratic and enjoying." [10]

He changed trains again at Still River. The broad reaches of the Nashua Valley, the ten-foot perpendicular banks of the Nashua River, even the seclusion, suggested Concord, magnified, intensified. He had seen nothing to compare with this spot since stopping here four days earlier. Here, he thought, one might live and dream one's time away. [11]

At home again on Main Street, one could neither live nor dream. Ellen was lame, and coughed much of the time. Rosa, the Welsh maid, packed up and vanished. Ellen was left with all the housework, the care of three children, and the sewing she must finish before her confinement in June. [12] Channing's actions suggest that he underestimated her sickness. He exploded more often now, forgetting what he had noted down about the futility of kicking and making wry faces. The children exhausted his patience. He suspected that their mother had been teaching them to hate him. [13] Mrs. Fuller was on hand presently, to help with the sewing;

then was added a new domestic, Irish and stupid.[14] At times the family included Eugene Fuller's stepdaughter Henrietta, an epileptic who boarded at Miss Ripley's school.[15] The chattering and the clattering swelled to a crescendo.

How refreshing to take to the river and record another kind of chatter. "O the buttery bobolink, that buttery, larripu-larripu, buttery, buttery, scattery, wattery-pattery, lattery of his. . . . Squeerp and rip of the night-hawk, the latter sound is quite itself, like the smart ring of a top when 'tis let off the string." "Stake-drivers bulgy pump about one minute, a puddled song, an air of mire and water echoing from puddled depths. Am-puddle, em-puddlee, Um-pudlee —Om goodout." [16]

In May he took three days from his profession to plant corn, potatoes, squash, beans, peas, tomatoes.[17] Meanwhile he and Emerson were transplanting also, for they were composing a series of real and imaginary conversations among the Concord friends by lifting comment and experience from the journals of Emerson and Thoreau and seasoning the mixture with old learning and fresh wit. Channing was to do most of the editing; Emerson would contribute not only much of the text, but also whatever money might be needed to publish it.[18] Alcott, hearing a sample, believed it promised "an entertainment as elegant and racy as anything in modern literature." [19]

Emerson was becoming earthier these days, and a merrier man than ten years before. Channing thought back to the nervous and frail philosopher who had welcomed him to Concord, and marked the contrast. In those days Emerson had even smoked languidly, fingering his cigar delicately and not much caring whether it was lighted, while Channing outpuffed him two to one. But better health and a more public life had changed the man. Having always loved cor-

diality in others, Emerson was warmer now himself.* He
and Channing spoke a common tongue, spiced with puns
and whimsies. As the two waited out a shower under a
tree, Emerson remarked he had had his house slated, but
that it was easier to slate the house than the owner. He
added that one side of it was made of gold, to judge by
the cost.[20] But their talk was not all banter. On a day
when they walked out to Walden, Channing jotted, "Sex
goes into everything." [21] This was three years before the
birth of Sigmund Freud.

Giovanni Eugene Channing, Ellery's fourth child, arrived
on June 23. Named for two uncles, one of whom (the
Marchese d'Ossoli) he would never see, the baby was accorded a welcome as mixed as his appellation. Wentworth
Higginson sent his best wishes on the arrival of "the little
gentleman with so many n's and g's in his name." [22] On the
24th Channing penciled in his book: "A new boy yesterday,"
following the note with comments on railroad, rain, and
insects.[23] Later he crossed out "A new boy." One can imagine in this a symbolic act of necromancy, as two centuries
earlier he might have melted the wax image of an enemy.
If he so intended it, it was a sardonic whimsy, from which
he would have been the last to expect results; and, indeed,
little Eugene refused to disappear. Channing's problems
were not to be so easily solved.

One of these problems was financial. Dr. Channing had
always been his main support, and had gradually increased
the allowance as the family grew; but the present—and highest—figure was only $400 a year. Additional income seldom
exceeded $100.[24] Occasionally there were windfalls: on

---

* These comments on Emerson's development are a paraphrase
of notes on a loose leaf in one of Channing's notebooks. At the end
of the manuscript is written in ink: "This is a note on Emerson by
Ellery Channing by about 1858." Whatever the exact date, the change
was presumably observable by 1853.

May 20, a month before Eugene's birth, Ellery acknowledged a gift of $200 from Sam Ward, which, he said, had
saved him from bankruptcy.[25] But relief of this sort was
only temporary, and the chronic anxieties returned.

Channing kept his life as sweet as possible by daily excursions, usually with Thoreau or Emerson, seldom with
more than one companion at a time. Under an oak where
he had once composed some verses, he reminded himself
that all had since changed for the better. "Even if embar-
rassed life is better as it grows older. Thus it is like
cheese." [26] He passed a week in Boston, calling on Alcott,
conversing on literature and life, running through Alcott's
"Collections" and making suggestions both shrewd and
witty, proving himself the best of company.[27]

This year the dog days came early; George Minott, the
farmer across from Emerson's house, called it "seltry"
weather. On certain afternoons the world fairly smoked,—
drowsy afternoons made for locusts and cuckoos. Yet Channing noted that July 24 was "a day of fabulous summer
beauty. Landscape and seasons have never proved a failure
or a mortification. The sun is yet hot enough, the sky clear
enough and all in the right trim. So much will I leave here
behind me in favor of life beyond my bones. These pretty
things, skies, trees and flowers are here for my pleasure.
No matter then in how mean a house, how dirty or ill-
surrounded. Outdoors is my real parlor and kitchen, and
bravely swept and cleaned. Let the old shed I live in overnight, the rat-trap I shelter in with its mouldy boards, rot
and decay." [28]

The rattrap he sheltered in was soon to be sprung. Early
in October Ellen spoke to him with cool resolution. She had
decided to leave, and to take the children with her. He
knew that this threat was no idle one. He was shocked.
He had not wanted this; nor, he was sure, had he deserved

it. To him it seemed fiendish—to rob a man of his own children—flesh of his flesh! Channing's nature, to which he had been ever faithful, rose and cried out in agonized protest.

Perhaps he was surprised when she relented a little, offering to make one last trial, at least until spring. He felt too unhappy to talk with her about it at present, he said; they would discuss it later. Ellen stayed on. Her husband, remembering the cool, passionless determination of her voice, tried to be gentle. For a fortnight or so, he *was* gentle.[29] He made efforts in other directions also. When his father offered him a new suit of winter clothes, he wrote a grateful acknowledgment—a rare attention that Dr. Channing scarcely expected.[30]

But Ellery's nature, that autocratic master, eventually shattered the ominous calm. Nature rebelled against a woman who cost so much money; who said she was leaving and yet remained; who tried to hush him before the children. Nature released the furies one day at the dinner table, driving him stamping to the kitchen, where he declared he would take his meals from this time on.[31]

It was November. The notebook was forgotten. Like the world around him, Channing's heart was thoroughly chilled and dried. As he sat brooding in his little room, or plodded through the back lanes where none should meet him, his thoughts were too brown to be recorded.

He was in his room the day that Higginson drove up to the door and assisted Ellen into the carriage. With them went little Walter and the baby; Marnie and Itty had already been sent away. If their father sensed the preparations or heard the final shutting of the door, he gave no sign.[32] Even when Higginson returned to see him the next morning, Channing would speak no word about his wife, though he was civil enough, and spoke readily on subjects of no concern.[33] Perhaps it seemed to him that the effrontery of this wife-stealer, this kidnapper, was too enormous for an oral rebuke. When his guest had gone, he seized a pen and formally concluded another episode. He wrote:

Concord, Mass. Nov. 18, 1853

Sir

   I will consider it a great favor, if you will never call on me again.

Yours,
W. E. Channing

Rev. T. W. Higginson [34]

The poet who had yearned for a peaceful household had been granted his wish, and he had no liking for it. His two companions, a sickly puppy and a cat, seldom cut the appalling stillness. He had a new and rueful name for the house: it was his Templum Concordiae. From this temple he escaped, as before he had escaped from pandemonium. Some of his goings-out and comings-in reached Ellen's ears; we shall hear rumors of his outward life presently. As for the life within, our best approach is through his notebook.

On December 28 the snow swirled around the Main Street houses, and sifted between the window sashes. Housebound, Channing reached for the little book which had received only occasional jottings since July. To the paper he committed a day-long reverie, playing intermittently on three themes: the driving storm, the languid puppy, and his own forlorn condition:

Garret full of snow, almost all the doors take in some. Now, I should judge about 2 p.m. no abatement. Sometimes can barely see house opposite. Wind quite high, not a gale but a fresh breeze. Think I must now begin to go back to my old habits, old literary habits especially. Have nearly gone mad, with love, hate, misfortune, despair etc. ever since this book was given up. I am almost mad now; however I still live and must try to pick up the fragments of myself. What has occurred is worse than useless to mention. But after a R R accident and the people are enough killed some one goes round and picks up all the remnants of baggage, bodies, brats, etc; thus I must do; I must go round and pick up. I fear there is not much to save. Still, whatever there may be, I am determined shall be picked up. First place, old habits would be well. Storm increases opposite houses almost concealed. Out-door rides were a great aid, a great comfort; I will begin again with these. Next literature, poetry, prose, etc. What time did this snow begin. Milkman not coming having nothing to feed pup on, fear he will die, is sick, badly so; he can scarcely walk, etc. Reading, writing, walking and talking, the latter to myself, being quite alone now. . . . I have got a cat, but the mice and rats are gone. Starved out. Read all Byron's letters and journals this week. A singular man, flippant but *most* unhappy, not most, nothing like what I have been through but so at bottom, while I am *not* so at bottom, but only at top. I have thoughts which rack me. If I can keep these out I can live. Pup is quiet. He may die but I shall not disturb him. Tomorrow if it stops snowing some milk. . . . Wintry desolation used to affect me, does not now; have known real desolation, nothing but death to come. Dont think I can walk. . . . Storm increases, grows dark. Afterwards walkd to village. Not so bad out, an imaginary evil. . . . Fed the pup on sugar and water with breadcrumbs. . . .[35]

The next day:

I am calmer than yesterday. I get up every morning refreshed, a new man; the morning is new, so am I. Before night I usually fall back into a misery unnamable. But I might also remember the morning. Stillness of today great contrast from noise yesterday. I have notions continually of leaving here; and taking some new place in which to live. But they appear to be mere notions nothing more, light as dust. And mere notions are not very important when I wish to be carried away and dropt in a new place. . . . I am that no novel has ever described. Such solitude. Now six weeks of this, and might be so sixty years if I remain here. Ever the same. Only myself, no other human form. This is quiet outside, solitude, cheap living, absolute retirement, can make nothing of it yet. If a habit might find it not easy to break it. Different from last winter. O ciel. . . .[36]

The Inner Voice

(1853–1855)

Back in September, when the tensions and explosions had become unbearable, Ellen had sought the help of Wentworth and Mary Higginson. She had written also to Richard for a new explanation of her legal rights, and to Dr. Channing, begging him to come to Concord to advise her on a terrible situation. The poor old Doctor, always helpless where Ellery was involved, was bewildered by the vagueness of her note; he replied in two long letters to his daughter Mary, asking that she explain to Ellen the necessity for him to preserve neutrality, but that she assure Ellen of his love and financial help, whatever might happen. To the Higginsons, who sat down with her in Concord, Ellen laid bare the sorry picture of her household: Ellery's abusive language, his threats of physical violence, his moodiness, his neglect—from all of which she and the children suffered increasingly. To continue in this way was dangerous. Did the perils outweigh considerations of loyalty? Ellen wanted advice; the Higginsons prudently gave her their love and sympathy, but declined to make the fateful decision.[1]

For five more days she turned her problem over and over; finally her action was but the postponement of action. She feared Ellery, but even more she feared self-reproach unless she made one more try. She wrote to Dr. Channing, to Richard, to the Higginsons; and warned Ellery this would be the last attempt.[2]

Ellen thought this final test would endure until spring, at least. There were two weeks of relative calm. Gradually Channing's angry tone of voice returned, and there was a relapse to what seemed close to insanity.[3] Night after night Ellen could hear her husband prowling through the house. In terror she barricaded her door. On November 14 she talked with Higginson again. Realizing her fright, he urged her this time to leave. It was four days later that he came for her.

Even when she had resolved to go, she was full of solicitude for Ellery. "It so distresses me," she remarked to Higginson, "that only my side has been heard. Everybody befriends me; but he confides in no one. If he could only once ease his mind about me and say the worst things he has to say about me, it would relieve his mind so much; but he broods over it night and day in his chamber alone, and out walking, with all the intensity of his mind, and he must go mad unless some relief can be found." [4]

In Worcester Ellen tried to fashion a normal life for her children and herself. By early December, they had moved from the Higginsons' into rented rooms nearby,[5] where, she recalled to Wentworth later, "the children could throw a snowball at you as you shaved." [6] There was a better chance to restore a home feeling to the little family now that she was free from the irritations of the Concord house. The material problems were variously met: her mother sent knives, forks, and crockery, also sundry articles salvaged in Concord by Arthur Fuller because they were his mother's.[7]

From the Unitarian minister of Concord, the Reverend Barzillai Frost, Ellen received several boxes of personal goods which were specifically her own and the children's.[8] A promise from Dr. Channing of $300 a year, and more if needed, reduced her worries; even more than the money she welcomed the assurance that the Doctor sympathized and felt affection for her still.[9]

Yet, as she cooked and sewed and swept, she asked herself a thousand questions—questions distinct, but interlaced and overlapping. For very few did she have ready answers. All the questions were included in the one: What about the consequences?

Barely a week after Ellen had left Concord, there had come from Ellery a four-page sheet of brown paper which raised the legal issue. The top of page 1 had been torn off, as if for a fresh start. The new version began:

To Mrs Ellen K F. Channing. Concord Nov. 25, 1853
I command you as your husband, as you have left my bed & board without provocation to return forthwith with my children. I make this order absolutely & for the last time. I have never & I shall never consent to a separation between us, and in no case will I relinquish my rights to and in my children.
I am & have always been willing to do anything to make your life more agreeable to you here, & shall continue in that mind. Should you not accede to this perfectly reasonable & right request, I must then proceed to take those other steps which will be so painful to my children to yourself & to me. I advise you to leave your children for a day & to come here, & talk over this matter. Any day you may appoint I shall be here to see you.

W E Channing
It seems to me so totally out of your character to deliberately sit down to destroy a man, who has never done you an injury in his life, that I cannot believe it. I have never & in the presence of God I would say the same, done you an injury. I had never

even so much as faintly dreamed of a separation from you up to the moment last spring I believe, you first spoke of it.

But if I had done you all the injuries ever inflicted by the worst man who ever lived, what could they be compared with the injury, the living death you propose to me. To endeavor to deprive me of the only beings on earth for whom I have any fondness, or who are in any manner connected with me, to propose seriously to seize from a father his children, all his children, because you may think I have done *you* injuries, but great God! what has this to do with my children, beings who owe their life to me, who are mine as much as they are yours, to become the deliberate murder of your husband's peace of mind, to make the earth a living grave to him, a man who has done all on earth that he could do, for you, & to set yourself up in judgment over me. Why did you not poison me, or stab me, or kill me outright, or do you think that I can live here and die by inches? And to think that you can have advised with strangers over this, with your mother or brothers, over my death, over this cruel, horrible unnatural murder of a man who has never consciously injured you in his life, & you a woman, one who values herself upon her heart. There must be a God, there must be justice, there must be for horrible crimes a horrible end. I do not wish to bring upon my children the awful recollection of their father's violent death, I do not wish to bring them into Courts of Justice, but I am innocent man, & to have my whole mind and heart destroyed without fault is too horrible to contemplate.[10]

A fortnight later Ellen received a note from George M. Brooks, a Concord lawyer. "Your husband," he began, "has called upon me in relation to his legal rights as to the custody of his children." Brooks gave her a week to bring the family back to Concord. After that time, Mr. Channing would resort to legal measures for their recovery.[11]

Of Ellen's reply to her husband I shall say more later. She rejected his command, assured him that she had confirmed the legality of her action, and reminded him that her departure had not been "without provocation." [12] Nevertheless she strengthened her defenses. With the approval of her brother Richard, then a practicing attorney, Wentworth Higginson consulted Judge Charles Allen * of Worcester, who wrote a reply to Brooks.[13] Dr. Channing also addressed his own protest to the Concord lawyer. He told Brooks that he was reducing Ellery's allowance by half, that his son had no visible means of supporting the family.[14]

On the remote chance that Ellery might precipitate a court battle, Higginson traveled to Concord and took depositions from several intimates of the Channings: Miss Clara Cutter and Mrs. Thoreau, neighbors; Minot Pratt, a former neighbor; Ann Mohan, a housemaid; Henrietta Fuller, Ellen's niece. All testified to Channing's unfitness as a father, and supplied incidents in evidence.[15] Richard added to the collection a long statement from his mother, who of all the relatives was most familiar with the problem. She mentioned Channing's slighting remarks about religious institutions and the religious instruction of children; she also stressed his irritability, recalling specific occasions of anger or petulance. She called him "as unsuitable . . . to have charge of children as anyone I ever knew." [16]

There may have been a conference between lawyers Allen and Brooks. Perhaps the correspondence was enough to convince Brooks that he had no case. This is certain: Channing did not make good his threats.

So much for the law. Another chain of consequences concerned the heart, and this was harder to deal with. In the security of Worcester, Ellen pondered his formal demand that she return, and Channing's informal, pleading postscript. Her reply was severe, but, like his letter, was softened

---

* Probably Charles Allen (1797–1869), later Chief Justice of the Superior Court for the Commonwealth.

by an afterthought. It was as if a voice had whispered to each in turn: "Come now. You have loved too deeply to let it go at that."

Ellen's letter stated clearly that her decision was irrevocable, that if Ellery acquiesced quietly he might still preserve some relationship with the children. As for herself: "Farewell and forever, if anything must come between us in the future it will be thro others. I cannot write again." After a formal signature came the postscript: "I wish to add this, that it is only while you assume this antagonistic attitude that I decline to write to you. . . ." [17]

There was no immediate solution to the problem of the heart.

During the weeks that followed, Ellen received from Concord, by several grapevines, a series of reports on Channing and his activities. The night after her departure, he and Henry Thoreau had "had a jubilee in the front parlor"; * at least once he had been invited to dinner by Mrs. Thoreau; he dined regularly with the Emersons; he went boating, as usual, with Henry; he was on his good behavior, and had treated with civility certain people to whom he had formerly been rude. [18] When Channing took the nine o'clock train to Boston on December 21, Mr. Wild, the station agent, telegraphed the fact to Higginson in accordance with a prearrangement; Wentworth wished to be on guard against a kidnapping whenever Channing left Concord. [19] The children were not disturbed, and no alarm was sounded on their father's later departures.

In April Ellen learned that Channing had left for a two-week visit to the Tappans' in Lenox; [20] soon afterwards, that he had packed "all his wearable clothes" in an old trunk, had authorized the washerwoman, Mrs. Murray, to

* This was Mrs. Barzillai Frost's report to Mrs. Fuller. Mrs. Frost may have seen or heard from the street something resembling gaiety, but certainly the joy did not run deep.

admit to the house some prospective tenants, and had said he might not return for six months.[21]

The first of April Ellen had moved to Dorchester, renting a house on Adams Street near Harrison Square. The children reveled in the country atmosphere. There was a barn nearby, with cows which Marnie learned to curry and to milk; and baby Eugene at twelve months could tell what the calf said. The children liked their school. Agreeable neighbors came to call. Life, it seemed, might still offer Ellen something good—perhaps even serenity.[22]

She drew strength from the fact that her course of action had the unanimous backing of her relatives. William Henry Fuller, living in Cincinnati and quite unacquainted with the problem, had at first expressed doubt; but even he conceded that the separation must be for the best if Channing's relatives approved it. William thereupon supplemented Ellen's slender income with a gift of $500, payable over a two-year period. "I trust that there will be no reconciliation, that would be ridiculous and I for one should lose all sympathy with her," he said.[23]

Such calmness of mind as Ellen achieved was interrupted from time to time by letters from her husband. All were lovesick and melancholy. One of them asked her for the return of her picture. Another, an unsigned fragment, had been written at the Burnet House in Cincinnati, opposite the rectory where they had been married. He had just arrived after a depressing visit to Niagara; he thought he might suffer less in a large hotel. Perhaps he would go farther west; he was undecided. The next letter was from Concord, where a note awaiting him from Ellen had apparently—whatever its intention—stirred up both memory and hope. The sight of the children's toys lacerated his heart. He had learned, too, of a visit she had paid to Concord in his absence to pick up some books and clothing; that had brought her nearer to him, and revived the ache.[24]

The immediate effect of these letters was to strengthen Ellen's resolve. Indeed, for the first time on record she reproached herself for having married him. Exasperated by Channing's self-deception, she poured out the feelings of the moment to Higginson, the one person in whom she felt she always could confide. "Oh! Wentworth how terribly have I expiated the one hasty action of my youth—giving to this man my womans troth, when wisely given it would have yielded such fruit of grace and progress toward heavenly wisdom. . . ."[25] The possibility of reconciliation seemed remote indeed.

Time brought partial healing to both body and mind. Even Channing became gentler in his pleading.[26] Ellen was able increasingly to focus her attention on other concerns. There was Barbara Channing's return from England. There were excursions to Milton, to Nahant, to William Fuller's new home in Lincoln. There was a visit from Ellen's brother Eugene, who gave her two birthday books: *Sunny Memories* and *Walden.* ("Each charming in their rather opposite styles," she said. "I really enjoy Thoreau's book—it is so thoroughly characteristic, and fresh.")[27] Snow fell, and Christmas approached. She wrote to the Higginsons: "This preparing for Christmas brings last winter so vividly before me. ah how sad I felt then—now comparatively cheerful. . . . God bless you and us all, and if not a merry Christmas a thankful one."[28]

Through the winter her tranquillity increased, and with the spring she felt her energy reviving. With returning health came thoughts of Ellery, more insistent than before, and strangely different. Though she remembered distinctly all that had passed, the terror was gone; in its place was an aching tenderness. For weeks she dreamed of him, by night and by day. At last the realization pierced her: she was still in love. For a time she said nothing about it—even to Wentworth Higginson. She needed to be certain. Any move toward her husband must be a lonely one, unblessed by those who had saved her once. She wondered how she could ever explain to them—to the Higginsons, her mother, brothers, friends. But that would be a problem for the future. She must proceed cautiously, one step at a time.

Convinced that she loved her husband as tenderly as on their wedding day, she finally wrote him of her feeling. She assured him of her love, of her wish to be once more his friend and confidante, of her desire, as always, to have the children think kindly of him. But she reminded him of his behavior which for a time obscured her love, and expressed fear that the old difficulties would arise if they attempted life together. He replied with joy and humility. Through suffering he had learned such wisdom, he felt they could be safely reunited. He said it in many ways, in several letters, before she wrote again.

This time she gave a little ground, but was unyielding on the main issue. They were not yet ready for reunion. If he believed he had mistreated her in their life together, he was merely accepting her word; she knew he had no memory of it, and that boded ill for a new attempt. Other conditions, too, were unfavorable: the children were even noisier now; there was as little money as ever; she was still too weary to be entertaining. Then she sketched the outline of a workable relation: he might come to call, for a few hours at a time, and so maintain an acquaintance with the children; he might draw even closer to them as they grew up; in the meantime, she would write him as fully and frequently as he desired.

For weeks no answer came; Ellen almost stopped expecting one. Eventually the postman brought it—in mid-July.*

* Although this was the month of Channing's second visit to Cape Cod with Thoreau, there is no evidence that Ellery ever discussed his family problems with his companion or that Thoreau ever offered advice on these matters.

As she read it, all resistance crumbled, though that fact she did not wholly recognize. With all defenses down, she was still to debate with Higginson and with herself the issue of surrender.

Channing's letter was sad, gentle, submissive. She longed to put his head on her heart, and to mother him.

To withhold her feelings any longer from Higginson would be neither loyal nor prudent. Furthermore, she thought she wanted advice. She wrote him in detail, going back to the season when Channing first began to haunt her day and night. She desperately tried to be objective as she retraced her course and described their correspondence. She balanced the alternatives. "The ghosts of terrible recollections rise up and I know that I now possess for myself outward repose, for my children freedom; shall I must I is it Gods will that I exchange these for a life which may be better and I think it would be, for if I go back, or am united to him again it must be for aye; there can be no second separation, except by death. I cannot see the end, but I prophecy it, I have a foreshadowing that I shall take him home again, not now but sometime."

She closed with a plea for guidance:

Dear good Wentworth you are the only being in the world on whose judgment I rely, and I do on yours, and have written this brief record of a life for you to read, and to write me upon. You may or may not show it to Mary—I think you had better not—she cares so much for me and has suffered so much in her sympathy for me, that I know she would as my mother does think it terrible to try this life again—but you feel and yet judge quietly which is the aid I want from you. As yet my own judgment is mute and says nothing, and so I know thus far I am to wait; till the inner voice shall be heard. Dear Wentworth, my dear friend how I love and value you I can never express.[29]

The next day Marnie wrote the Higginsons that Mother was quite sick.[30]

Of Higginson's reply we have only a line which Ellen quoted in her acknowledgment some three weeks later. "I thank you very much for your good and strong words," she said, "and I shall read them many times. I shall as you desire me endeavor 'to think calmly considerately and free from fluctuating emotions.' " She could agree to all he urged; she would not act until she was convinced the time had come. But from her letter it was obvious that the question was no longer whether, but when. Her lighter spirits were reflected in a breezy postscript to Mary, brimming with gossip. A reference to her thirty-fifth birthday was only semisobering: "Only think Mary you and I have reached half of that venerable age allotted to man, and now 'we've clumb the hill,' I suppose we 'maun totter down,' or tumble down, I do not know which." [31]

About September first the inner voice spoke to Ellen conclusively, and she broached her plan to her brothers. There is no record of their first remarks. Presumably Arthur's phrasing was an understatement when he told Eugene that Ellen's decision was "a step we can none of us advise." [32] William uttered something unpleasant which he later retracted.[33] Richard drew up a legal instrument to protect Ellen in the event of another separation.

This was an agreement between William Ellery Channing of Concord and a trustee acting on behalf of Channing's wife; it assured her of the children, the household goods, and half of her husband's income.[34] Close to midnight on September 18, Ellen composed a brief message to Higginson, telling him of her decision and begging him to accept the part of trustee. "Ellery feels very badly about signing it," she added, "and has not made up his mind that he will, but I think he will, for I believe that we shall lead a truer and better life." She closed with a wistful plea, "Dear W. I hope you will love me." [35]

Higginson's reply was cold. He had received a copy of the document, and wished to study it carefully. He would probably "be willing to undertake the charge, for the children's sake." [36] Not for her sake, but only for the children's —the distinction, so carefully implied, cut deeply. Yet she who had predicted her own decision might well have forecast also the exhaustion of Higginson's patience. Not long before, he had warned her frankly that if she returned to Channing she would be "half-consciously sacrificing the happiness of . . . the children's lives to the magnetism of a personal passion." [37]

Nevertheless the paper was duly signed by both parties, and there was a cordial exchange of notes between Channing and Higginson. [38] Ellery and Ellen resumed their family life, in Dorchester. A letter from Ellen softened Wentworth's manner; he wrote back with sympathy and affection. One of his paragraphs may well have spoken the thoughts of all the Fuller and Channing relatives:

It may be that you may soon satisfy us that we are mistaken and that your judgment, so often tested, is good here also; you are making an effort for a great end, though with a great risk; and you cannot suppose that any pride of opinion would prevent us from owning the truth. At any rate it will not be so; for I never wished more to find my first fears mistaken. [39]

Redemption

(1855–1856)

Ellen's brother Arthur was a guest preacher on October 14, 1855, in one of the Dorchester churches. On his way home he stopped at the Adams Street house to see the Channings. Ellen was there, and her brother found her "apparently very tranquil and even happy." Equally surprising, and most gratifying to Arthur, was the reason for Channing's absence. Not only had he gone to church, but he had gone for *all day*. It was apparent that Channing had entered on a new life.[1]

Both husband and wife were determined to make the marriage work. To this end the new home in Dorchester was more favorable than any return to scenes of past unhappiness. Besides, there were tenants in the Channing house in Concord—a young schoolteacher, Frank B. Sanborn, who with his sister had taken rooms there the previous spring.[2]

Though Ellen's lift of spirits made illness bearable, her physical health showed no improvement. Her cough persisted; once more she was pregnant. The relief that had followed her crucial decision, and the exemplary behavior of her husband, might otherwise have brought a lasting serenity. But she was oppressed by forebodings, which the older children knew and shared. When Richard Fuller's two tiny youngsters were left motherless, Ellen wrote to her brother: "My health is so uncertain that my two little girls never feel quite free from anxiety, and their dread of losing their mother is a realization to me that it would be far greater to them now than in infancy." [3]

Channing elected Christmas Day for carrying out an important personal mission in New Bedford. This was a visit to Daniel Ricketson, the Quaker littérateur, whom he had met in September when Ricketson was Thoreau's guest in Concord. Ricketson had known Thoreau only since the publication of *Walden* in August of the previous year; he had been so captivated by the book that he had felt he must meet the author. The attraction was partly due to the fact that Ricketson himself boasted a "shanty," a hideaway on the lawn of his ample house. In this retreat he could smoke his pipe cozily with his most intimate friends. The correspondence between Ricketson and Thoreau developed a firm friendship between the two even before the men met. They saw each other first on Christmas Day of 1854, when Thoreau arrived at Brooklawn, the Ricketson home, on his new friend's invitation. Ricketson was returning that visit at the time Channing made his acquaintance in September of 1855.

That first sojourn in Concord was for Ricketson a memorable experience. One of his desires had been to meet Channing, whom Thoreau had mentioned frequently. Ellery in person measured up to Thoreau's reports of him; he seemed to Ricketson the ideal companion with whom to smoke a pipe and, in Ricketson's language, to "feelosophize." Ricketson gave up his plans for a second visit in October when he learned that it would be impossible to feelosophize by Channing's wood fire.

Thoreau did his best to persuade Ricketson that Concord was Concord still, even without Channing; failing in this, Thoreau went to New Bedford for some autumn rambles with his friend. On his return he urged Channing also to visit Brooklawn, and the Christmas excursion followed soon after. As Ricketson opened the door to greet him, Channing pointed to the side, saying, "That's your shanty"; and minutes afterwards host and guest were puffing away in front of the shanty fireplace.[4]

This smoky session was a prelude to many more. In February, 1856, no doubt with the help of Ricketson, Channing was appointed an assistant editor of the New Bedford *Mercury,* and took a room in the city. It was delightful to exchange his rented quarters for the pungent atmosphere of Ricketson's shanty, and Channing walked out to Brooklawn often—in some weeks making several visits.

At the *Mercury* office, the new editor's duties were varied, and once more his writings were anonymous. He wrote editorials and news articles, poems and reviews, probably dipping into a reservoir of previously unpublished verse. It is impossible to identify all his work, but the issues of 1856 are frequently enlivened by sardonic quips that have the ring of the genuine Channing. For example:

A Fat Poet.—According to the tax-list of the town of Cambridge, Mr. Longfellow, the poet, is assessed to pay a tax of one thousand dollars this year. This is more money, according to all account, than most poets handle in the course of their lives.[5]

A good, bran-new broadcloth coat has been stolen from a Boston reporter, that hung up in the editorial office. This unparalleled event has caused intense excitement among the craft, not by reason of the theft, but the fact of ownership.[6]

Meanwhile, Channing mystified his friends by an impish reluctance to tell his whereabouts. He had already been secretive about the Dorchester address; when Thoreau, meeting him in Concord, had asked where he was living now, he had answered he did not know the name of the place. Even Ricketson was unable to learn the address of Channing's boarding house in New Bedford until Thoreau reported that a Mrs. Arnold had told Mrs. Emerson where it was, "and the latter thinks, though she may be mistaken, that it was at a Mrs. Lindsey's." *

We do not know how often Channing joined his wife and family in Dorchester, but the relationship seems to have been amicable. Apparently the visits were frequent.† Wentworth Higginson, who had doubted the authenticity of Ellen's "inner voice," was ready by November, 1856, to confess his amazement. "In justice to Ellery," he wrote, "I must say that his whole course since he went to New Bedford has been most creditable, and to me very astonishing." ᵗ

The Channings' fifth child, Edward, was born on June 15, 1856, a month prematurely. Ellen never regained her strength. Added to the cough was an internal inflammation which the doctors could not positively diagnose, but the effects of which were disheartening to her family.⁸ The children were put out to board in Milton,⁹ though Marnie was soon recalled to be her mother's "back and legs." Free from household duties, Ellen lay, or sat, throughout the summer—at Dorchester, then in a little rented room in Rockport,

* Anna and Walton Ricketson, *Daniel Ricketson and His Friends,* 3–60, *passim.* According to Sanborn, Mrs. Benjamin Lindsey, wife of the *Mercury* publisher, "was a distant cousin of the Channings, through the Sedgwicks of Berkshire." See Sanborn, "William Ellery Channing and Daniel Ricketson," New Bedford *Mercury,* Aug. 7, 1907.

† In the article noted above, Sanborn says that Channing "seems for a time to have passed up and down on the trains between New Bedford and Harrison Square several times a week."

then at Aunt Susan Fuller's in Lowell.* There was no longer anything to do but wait. When, in mid-September, Richard invited her to spend the coming month in Wayland, she said her visit must be earlier and shorter. She hoped by October to be settled in her winter quarters.[10]

As she waited, languidly, for an October that would never come, she found it harder to hold a pen and harder even to speak the messages which Marnie would write down for her. Her life was all within, and we can only guess how her mind was occupied. Certainly there was cause enough for apprehension, especially when she thought of her children, even then almost beyond her reach. But fear and regret may well have coalesced with a calming sense of satisfaction. That bond of love, so strong among the Fullers, which had made Marnie at twelve into a patient nurse, which had inspired such generous gifts and invitations from her brothers, and even forgiveness from William—this was cause for gratitude. As for Ellery the unpredictable, about whom only she had predicted rightly—there too must be love, the kind that one builds faith upon; for Ellery was fulfilling promises, earning a salary under conditions which he had formerly avoided, making regular payments to support little Edward,[11] justifying the action that had freed her conscience of its burden, astonishing the Higginsons and the Fullers. For the first time in many years, Ellen was proud of her husband.

She had pinned her faith to the redemption of her marriage; in fact, she had given her life for it. Perhaps, as she drifted into the shadow, she felt a momentary glow of victory.

* Susan Adams Fuller was the widow of Ellen's Uncle Elisha, who had practiced law in Lowell and Worcester.

The Lonely Road
(1856–1891)

Ellen died at Dr. Channing's house on September 22. Whether her husband was with her at the end and whether he stood afterwards beside her grave in Mount Auburn Cemetery must be left to conjecture. If he attended the service, it was the last family rite in which he joined. He would soon almost entirely forget that he was a father.

The relatives filled the vacuum as well as they could. Marnie went to live with the Higginsons. Walter became the responsibility of the Fullers, particularly Arthur and Richard. Caroline and Eugene remained with their grandfather and Aunt Barbara.

Dr. Channing took charge of little Edward, too; but for the first three years the child lived with a shoemaker's family in South Abington. The wife had nursed him almost from birth, when his survival seemed unlikely; and the Channings were glad to have her continue as a foster mother through his babyhood. On stopping to see him in South Abington, one of the relatives was surprised to find the baby lying in a drawer stuffed with shoe findings, and contentedly sucking on a lobster claw.[1]

Ellery seems to have toyed with the idea—briefly—of keeping his children with him. In November, 1856, he wrote a letter from his Dorchester address to Ricketson.[2] In it he asked whether there might be a house near New Bedford suited to his needs—which included proximity to schools and to a church, "old fashion Unitarian" preferably. But he did not pursue the project. If the relatives refused to let him take his own children, which is quite possible, he apparently acquiesced quietly—and probably with a sense of relief.

Meanwhile, he remained on the *Mercury* staff, but found more and more time for rambles in Concord. He took a vacation of at least twelve days in April of 1857,[3] and that summer he stretched a leave to something like two months.[4] His employment cannot be said to have terminated; it just tapered off. Ricketson, in whose shanty Channing had smoked his pipe two or three times a week in 1856, saw him less often thereafter. To be sure, Channing was frequently on hand during Amos Bronson Alcott's visit of a fortnight in the spring of 1857; and it was during that gathering of feelosophers that Thoreau danced and sang in the parlor, stepping on Alcott's toes, and inspiring Ricketson to commemorate the performance in verse.[5] That same year it was Channing who brought to Brooklawn the news of Thoreau's long beard, which, though "terrible to behold," improved his appearance. (Ricketson questioned whether a long beard was suitable for a short man.)[6] Twice in late 1858 Ricketson found Channing in the *Mercury* office; but even between these two occasions, some five weeks apart, Channing was walking with Thoreau to Walden and Fairhaven Hill.[7]

He tried feebly to keep contact with his children. In January, 1858, he wrote to his son Walter, regretting that he could not entertain both Walter and Eugene in Concord, and promising the gift of a watch. "You know how I am situated," he said, "deserted by those who should have cherished me and having no home for you. . . . I feel badly at not having visited Eugene and must go down this week. You have gone into Boston to live by your own choice and as you have taken up that way of life, I trust you will find it good for you. I wonder how you ever got admission into it." [8] This to an eight-year-old.

On one occasion—the date is unknown—he took a train to Salem, registered at a hotel, and hired a horse and buggy to take him out to Curzon's Mill. There he found the person he was seeking—Mary Curzon, the second daughter of that idyllic family—still beautiful, still vivacious, still single. He asked her squarely whether she would marry him.

"Ellery," she replied, "you have killed off one wife, but you certainly won't kill me."

Channing said that he was sorry she felt that way, but that the offer stood; he would go back to Salem and wait at the hotel until she replied favorably.* No word came from her; and eventually he returned to Concord.

He now had the Main Street house quite to himself, Sanborn and his sister having moved in April, 1858, from their rented rooms.[9] No longer the wanderer, from now on Channing lived at home most of the time. His rare excursions were for a few days at most.

Counting 1858, there were to be four good years of comradeship with Thoreau; and at the age of forty, neither man had reason to sense any impending doom. For Thoreau, overnight trips were frequent and the company was varied.

---

* Approximately fifty years later she told this story to her grandnephew John P. Marquand. She added, "I dare say that Ellery is waiting at the hotel in Salem still, because I have never sent for him." (John P. Marquand, "A Hearsay History of Curzon's Mill," *Atlantic,* CC [November, 1957], 84–91.)

In June of '58 he climbed Monadnock with his friend H. G. O. Blake of Worcester, passing two nights on the rugged slopes.* In July he visited the White Mountains with Edward Hoar. But it was Channing who tramped the sands of Cape Ann with Thoreau in September.[10] In August, 1860, they camped together on Monadnock, an expedition of five nights. They made their ascent on a drenching day, and found Thoreau's old campsite in a cloud. Henry swiftly raised a hut of spruce boughs that won his companion's praise; then built before the door a fire that dried out their clothes by bedtime. In the morning the peak above them shone olive-brown as the first rays of the sun struck the wet lichens; and Channing named it Mount of Olives. Thoreau made extensive notes on birds, plants, and rocks, and on the human visitors who spent so much time engraving their names with hammers and cold-chisels that they missed the view.[11]

In the spring of 1861, when Thoreau was advised to travel west for his health's sake, he invited Channing to go with him. Ellery vacillated, and then said No. After Thoreau had substituted young Horace Mann as a companion, Channing hinted he might still join them at Niagara Falls. He did not do so, and Thoreau was disappointed.[12] But both before and after that fruitless trip, Ellery's solicitude exceeded anything he had ever accorded his own family. "Channing has looked after me very faithfully," Thoreau wrote to Ricketson; "says he has made *a study of my case* and knows me better than I know myself." [13]

---

* Canby says Channing went with Thoreau on this 1858 trip, but that appears to be an error. In a letter to Ricketson on June 30, Thoreau implies that he has had only a fleeting glimpse of Channing recently, and speaks of his Monadnock excursion with Blake. In 1876 Channing wrote in his "Monadnoc" journal some reminiscences of his first trip, which he dated August, 1858; but the events are those of August, 1860.

Ricketson's own relations with Channing were less happy. On a visit to Thoreau in November, 1859, he had called on Ellery and smoked a pipe with him. Two days later, making a farewell call after breakfast, he was amazed when Channing suddenly withdrew without explanation to his attic room, leaving the guest in the kitchen. Again in Concord in 1861, Ricketson saw Channing in the street, but avoided speaking in order to escape embarrassment.[14] Apparently the men never met again, although Ricketson sent cordial greetings from time to time through mutual friends, and in 1868 Channing went with the Ricketson children, Anna and Walton, to look at Thoreau's hut, by then removed to the Clarke farm on the Estabrook road.[15]

By the close of 1861 it was apparent that Thoreau's health was past recovery. Yet during those final months, when he lay on his day-bed in the parlor and received his friends, his senses were so keen, and his mind was so playful, it was hard to believe what sober judgment indicated. Channing, who probably looked in on him every day, was as unprepared as any for the blow. When confronted by an inconvenient fact, Ellery had habitually turned his face the other way. It is unlikely that he then admitted, even to himself, that Henry would die; though Thoreau himself spoke freely of the inevitable, and said to Channing, "It is better some things should end." [16]

The day came—May 6, 1862—when Channing must accept the actuality. It was he who walked to Alcott's and broke the unhappy news.[17] Certain decencies must be observed; it was Channing's duty and privilege to have a part in them. He wrote four stanzas for the funeral service; not good poetry, but born of honest grief. These were "plaintively sung" [18] at the simple rites on May 9, and in the coffin were placed three quotations which Channing had selected.

Hail to thee, O man, who art come from the transitory
place to the imperishable.[19]

Gazed on the heavens for what he missed on earth.[20]

I think for to touch also
The world which neweth everie daie,
So as I can, so as I maie.[21]

Henceforth his one absorbing interest was to be the memory of Henry Thoreau. It is doubtful that he made any vows,
or realized that here at length was the challenge that could
wake his dormant energies. Yet in the years ahead, his talents, which were considerable, would never yield anything
better than the tributes he would pay his friend. In his
zeal to recreate the past, and the personality that had given
it meaning, he was to discover a use for the future, too—
which otherwise held little interest for him.

Almost immediately Channing was faced with an opportunity to serve his dead friend as an editor of the unpublished manuscripts. Henry's sister Sophia, who controlled
the papers, guarded them jealously; for her, as for Channing, to handle them and to arrange them for publication
was a reverential process, a privilege that could be accorded
only the most sympathetic friends. Sophia would have been
happy to remain the sole editor; but being quite unskilled
in the craft, she turned for help to Henry's closest companion. Channing himself was ill fitted for the exacting
demands of such a task, but he had been an editor of sorts,
and he could give his heart to the project. Together they
produced *The Maine Woods* in 1864, and *Cape Cod* the
next year. Two parts of *The Maine Woods* had appeared in
Thoreau's lifetime; only the Allegash and East Branch excursion required editing, and in this account the editors mis-
placed one day's journey in such a way as to confuse any

attentive reader.[22] But the essence of the work was quite independent of map or calendar, and could not be seriously
harmed by rearrangement. Sophia's choice of Channing as a
collaborator a second time was natural; their edition of *The
Maine Woods* was being well received, and Channing had
shared many of the experiences recorded in *Cape Cod*. On
this volume he and Sophia did a workmanlike job. Whether
the same partnership prepared *A Yankee in Canada, with
Anti-Slavery and Reform Papers* is unknown. Again, the
choice of Channing would have been obvious, since he and
Henry had visited Quebec together.

As public interest in Thoreau's work developed, there appeared to be a ready market for the journals. Doubtless
Channing was eager to present and to interpret to the
world this record of a mind and of a way of life that he had
known so intimately. The story may be true that in 1874,
after he had used parts of the journals in his biography,
Sophia threatened to put the manuscripts in the Public
Library "so that Channing could not get at them," and
that thereafter he refused to speak to her.[23] But Sophia was
reluctant to trust the manuscripts to any editor, or her
brother's memory to any biographer. She refused permission
to James T. Fields and to Thomas Wentworth Higginson,
both of whom asked permission to edit the journals.[24] Regarding a biography, she could conceive of no one competent to write it. "Henry's character was so comprehensive
that I think it would take many minds to portray it," she
wrote to Ricketson.[25]

This rift between Channing and the Thoreaus was not
the first. He and Mrs. Thoreau had never cared much for
each other; and Channing is said to have begged Henry
sometimes to get her out of the house. On one occasion,
after Thoreau's death, she had spoken to Channing so sharply
that he broke off all relations; it required a visit to Concord
by the young Ricketsons to heal the breach. But Channing's

friendships blew hot or cold on short notice. Whenever he cut his old associates on the street, they could reasonably expect that—given time—the mood, like the weather, would change. Sometimes his neglect was a passing whim; occasionally it sprang from a resentment that only months or years could heal. His break with Bronson Alcott took two years to mend, and even then it was Mrs. Alcott whom Channing called on and to whom he addressed all remarks. But this wound had been deeper than most, for Alcott had actually ordered him from the house, being displeased by a piece of gratuitous advice.[26]

Channing had his tiff with Sanborn, too. During 1863 he wrote a biography of Thoreau running to one hundred thirty-four pages of manuscript, and offered it for publication to his former tenant, who had turned from schoolteaching to journalism and was editing a daily newspaper, the Boston *Commonwealth*. Sanborn copyrighted the manuscript, and agreed to publish it in weekly installments, beginning on December 25, 1863. But after the serial had appeared for several weeks, the editor cut it off abruptly. Angered, the author took back his biography and for a time completely abandoned the project. The *Commonwealth* serial was never resumed.[27]

In October, 1865, Channing sold the Main Street house.* Once too small for a poet and his family, it was now far too spacious for the poet alone. Moreover, the closeness to the Thoreaus and to the river had lost all importance in Henry's absence. The house itself, which he had once called a rattrap, was haunted by figures and voices from an unhappy past. No doubt these reminders were too insistent.

Yet Channing could not persuade himself to cut the cords completely. Several of Ellen's dresses hung in her chamber

---

* The property was conveyed on Oct. 17, 1865, to Frederic Hudson for $2,500. (Middlesex County Registry of Deeds, Vol. 959, pp. 101–2)

closet. He removed them carefully, carried them to his new home at 6 Middle Street, and hung them in another closet.*
This may have been sentiment, or it may have been the miserliness to which he confessed in his journal. He was an inveterate saver of trifles; under his bed, in 1867, were the fragments of an old trunk which he had knocked to pieces years before.[28]

The Middle Street house had been bought for Channing by his father.[29] For almost half a century, the Doctor had been trying to make up to his motherless boy for the deficiencies of heritage or training that had produced this eccentric life. Dr. Channing felt as responsible as ever—and as puzzled. He seldom saw his son; there was something pathetic about his efforts to maintain contact. To the Doctor, Ellen had been a dutiful and loving daughter; she had been a link between father and son. Now, apparently, communication was indirect and infrequent—except for the automatic monthly check on which Ellery had long depended. Perhaps the gift of a house was the Doctor's last desperate gesture of affection and conciliation.

Ellery had reason to favor this particular house. Although removed from its old location, and remodeled into a two-family dwelling, it had been the home of the Concord Academy, and later of the private school kept by the Thoreau brothers from 1838 to 1841. In these very rooms Henry had taught the classics to the older boys while John was leading their younger brothers in their games.[30] The surroundings were encouraging to the new career into which Channing now entered—that of the scholar.

This time there was none of the self-consciousness or the semihumorous dedication that had marked his earlier transi-

* Mrs. Chilton Cabot, Channing's granddaughter-in-law, remembered that the dresses were dropping apart from age when Channing left the Middle Street house in 1891. (Interview with Mrs. Cabot, Dec. 30, 1932)

tions from "profession" to "profession." This was a natural development which he himself may not have noticed at the start. He went to the woods less frequently these days, for he had lost his favorite walking comrade, and he was winded more quickly on the hills. So more and more he turned to books. For twenty-five years they would be his chief companions.

In February of 1867, after he had been on Middle Street for about a year, he started another journal; and for four months he seldom missed a day. Through the summer the entries grew infrequent; by September the impulse had run its course. Unlike the notebooks of the early fifties, in which he had jotted brief records of his rambles but had seldom generalized, the journal of 1867 received an extended series of essays on life and death, and of comments on his current reading. Where the little notebooks had served to extend his memory of sounds and sights, impersonally described, the new journal was subjective. The dominant theme is futility. It is the testimony of a lonely man, bereft of wife and family (whom, to be sure, he does not mourn), and of his dearest friend (whom he mourns throughout); a man for whom ambition, incentive, and hope are nearly dead. His comment on a neighbor reflects his prevailing mood:

Brooks Abel. Old Uncle Abel has died, a sort of stooping, half-witted, deaf, penurious booby, just about 80 years. I saw him a day or two since working at his woodpile and then nature came and cracked him on her thumb like a louse. . . . Uncle Abel never said a good word for anybody to my knowledge. He was very deaf and his wife was deafer and Pulsifer deafer than all—what a family, bawling their blockheadisms to each other. Uncle Abel, often shall I see thy ghost and next nature will come and set me on her thumb, come my little skipjack, here is apoplexy or paralysis, (numb palsy they call it in the country) or a fit, and crack—I shall be even as Uncle Abel was: saved, if not worse.[31]

Here also was Channing's wry comment on his own success:

That is my special function, the having and the being of opacity. Dull I came upon the planet, untalented, the one talent still in that tremendous napkin, out of which I have never been able to unwrap it and where it is still like to be for all I can discern thro its folds.

Still, I shall seek a little longer before I shut up the magic lens called opportunity and utterly hibernate, like the woodchuck whose tracks I do not see all the long winter thro. But every animal makes tracks, only some do not come into view. Why even I succeed in making tracks in the snow, and others in walking in them. Methinks, this is the greatest success I ever had in life.[32]

Yes, he would tarry a bit before he hibernated. For life had teased him with her riddles, and he still took pleasure in searching for the answers, though in his acid moods he would deny it. Also there was still much to be done to preserve the personality of Thoreau—although Channing would have insisted that duty was not involved here. He had remarked: "As to that moral sense, that idea of the duty and the like, of which so much is writ, I have never had any of it." [33] But it was satisfying to compose memorials to his friend, just as it was to lose himself in books. When he was so engaged, life was better than tolerable.

As for the reading, his comments in those eight months of 1867 suggest the range of his interests. The list is weighted with geography and history: Livingston's *Africa,* Barth's *African History,* someone on Palestine, another on Pompeii. From May 9 to June 4 he writes of nothing but the Franklin expedition to the Arctic, speculating, as he reads the published account, on the fate of Sir John and his men. He quotes St. Beuve, who quotes Lamartine; he alludes to Denham and Vamberg. He comments on an account of Lessing by Stater. He has read Thackeray's *English Humourists;* detesting the writer, he names also half a dozen other English authors whom he finds disagreeable, but has a word of faint praise for Johnson. More absorbing than these literati are the physicist Oken and the metaphysicist Hegel. He puts down his own bold guesses about the nature of light and about the inhabitants of the sun. He devotes three days of his journal to Carpenter's *Physiology*.

Also the ghost of Henry Thoreau saunters through these daily entries. Now and then Channing will visit their old haunts, for the habits of twenty years cannot be put off overnight. He will recall Henry's name for this bright, blowy weather between winter and spring. ("These are what H. called working days, days when activity, vitality, change become paramount.") [34] He will remember the path they used to follow around that pond and over that hill. Here, too, are Henry's thoughts and his ways of thinking:

I remember H. once said, as he spoke of some minute thing, I forget what, that the art of genius was to raise the little into the large. This was in one of the last times we were out together, near Flint's Bridge. . . .

H. was fond of making an ado, a wonder, a surprise of all facts that took place out-of-doors, but a picture, a piece of music, a novel did not affect him in this fashion. He exaggerated the permanence of everything but what men do and like all writers who have had literary success, necessarily deemed his own writing of special importance. It is well that some fail, or none would know what a trifle the best writing is. But this trait of exaggeration in H. was as pleasing as possible so far as his companion was concerned. Nothing was more delightful, than the enormous curiosity, the continued greenness, the effervescing wonder of this child of nature, glad of everything its mother said or did.[35]

This was an intimate comment, not yet for the public eye. But his other portraits of Thoreau were in the making, too.

In 1871 Sanborn edited and Emerson financed a blank-verse pastoral by Channing entitled *The Wanderer, a Colloquial Poem*. As on other occasions, Emerson put his prestige as well as his cash behind the venture, and wrote a preface—a friendly one, though needlessly defensive.

For this is the best of Channing's longer poems—the most fluent, the most coherent, the most pictorial. To be sure, there are flaws: the colloquial language is mingled with the archaic and the erudite; some sections are choked with bookish similes; there are neoclassical circumlocutions (the Great Glacier is the *polar host*). There are odd inversions, too, to meet the demands of meter. But all these faults, which also mark his earlier poems, appear in *The Wanderer* less often, while his merits are multiplied. Like Emerson, he has become more earthy; gone are the Transcendental abstractions; he now preaches a social gospel. There is nothing radical in his asking compassion for the poor, but he strikes a new note in advocating votes for women.

The three divisions—"Wood," "Mountain," and "Sea"—offer the poet occasion to reminisce in verse about the scenes of his excursions and the company he kept. Thinly veiled are the familiar Concord characters, with Thoreau to the fore in the subsections labeled "The Hermit" and "Henry's Camp." His lines on Henry at Walden fairly represent his more facile and unpretentious passages:

> True, the traditions of the race still ticked
> Like spiders in the web, shut in his ears;
> And still he heard that drumming in his dreams,
> And schemed reforms to agitate the earth
> With penny wisdom, and insure the peace.
> Yet oft he fed the titmice from his hand;
> And the old, cautious muskrat, who, behind
> This hermit's hut, had built himself a house,

Felt no alarm at him who daily left
An alms at his back door, and kept the faith.
When the short winter-days ran rapid out
If clear the air, he heard the small pond sing
Its well-known strains of pleasure and of praise,
As on the strings of an Aeolian lyre;
And saw the sentry pines that fringe the east
Erect their emerald tips along the eve,
While all the singular fibres of the pond
Kept on their whining music.[36]

Undoubtedly the felicitous lines owe something to the editor, and perhaps something to the sponsor also, who remarked about the poet's unexpected docility regarding changes. One happy result of their teamwork was the rapid sale of the edition, which according to Sanborn was nearly exhausted within a month.[37] The unsold copies were consumed by fire, probably in the great conflagration that swept Boston in 1872.[38]

Two years after *The Wanderer*, Channing performed the most useful single service of his life in the publication of *Thoreau, the Poet-Naturalist*. It was the first biography of his friend; and in the essentials it will keep its authority, for it sprang from the most primary of sources, an intimacy of twenty years. The living personality of Thoreau was known to only one other of his biographers—Frank Sanborn —and Sanborn was rather an acquaintance than a friend.

This is not to say that Channing's is the best biography by any other measurement than closeness to the subject and affection for him. Later writers have shown other facets of Thoreau's character, and offered sounder judgments. But all have used the information that only Channing could supply.

Some of the oddities of the work can be explained by the

method of production. Shortly after the modest success of *The Wanderer*, Sanborn proposed to Channing the publication in book form of the biography prepared in 1863, and with Channing's approval arranged with the firm of Roberts Brothers for an edition of 1,500 copies. The final manuscript was rather assembled than composed. "With the perversity of genius," says Sanborn, "Channing had gone over his first draft, omitting much, making portions of the rest obscure and enigmatical, but enriching it with the treasures of his recondite learning in mottoes, allusions, and numberless citations,—the whole without much method, or with a method of his own, not easily followed by the reader, who had not the guide-board of an index to help him out." [39] To the collection he added excerpts from his own notes, including passages from the journal of 1867, and selections from Thoreau's journals, from which, through the years, he had copied extensively. But this was not all. When the publisher discovered that the volume would be fifty pages short of the desired length, he called for more copy; and Channing obligingly supplied the need from the old "Country Walking" manuscript which he had contrived with Emerson and Thoreau from their journals in 1853. [40]

What came forth was not a chronological account, but a series of biographical essays, interspersed with imaginary dialogues in which the speakers address one another in elevated language—making hard work even of their wit. These conversations may fairly reflect the subject matter of the Concord walk-talks, but the phrasing is too mannered to carry conviction. More readable are the chapters for which Channing took full responsibility. He still employed the bushel-of-nuts style, but that certified his kinship to the other Transcendentalists.

The public vindicated Sanborn's judgment, and bought out the edition. Channing had a right to feel elated. By now inured to failure, he cannot have been indifferent to success. It must have pleased him, too, to know that he had tightened, even a little, Thoreau's grip on immortality.

Whatever Sophia Thoreau thought of the book, she disliked Channing's unauthorized use of the journals. Even Emerson was vexed, for the "Country Walking" interludes had included some of his unpublished verse; [41] but with Emerson no such petty annoyances could interrupt a friendship. Channing may have acted on a permission granted (or taken for granted) twenty years before; and Emerson may have recognized this likelihood. Moreover, Emerson's generous mind was already touched with haziness, and it is unlikely that he thought it through, or let it bother him for more than a passing hour.

Yes, Emerson could be counted on, and his hospitality was one of the dependables in life. Channing had a standing invitation to take tea with the family on Sundays. He was a guest on special days besides, including Thanksgiving, when the white house swarmed with grandchildren; [42] and often he was summoned there to greet a visiting celebrity. One of these was The Honourable Lyulph Stanley, who would later be the fourth Baron Stanley; to meet him Emerson produced Louis Agassiz and Wendell Phillips, along with Channing and Alcott.[43] Channing was also invited to share the company of Bret Harte, but flatly refused "any part in his reception, guidance, or dinner." [44]

The young poet Emma Lazarus, who would one day write the sonnet for the pedestal of the Statue of Liberty, was not yet famous when she visited the Emersons in 1876, but Channing joined in her entertainment. She found him "a pathetic, impossible creature, whose cranks and oddities were submitted to on account of an innate nobility of character." The portrait she drew of him in her journal is worth quoting fully:

Generally crabbed and reticent with strangers, he took a liking to me. The bond of our sympathy was my admiration for Thoreau, whose memory he actually worships, having been his constant companion in his best days, and his daily attendant in the last years of illness and heroic suffering. I do not know whether I was most touched by the thought of the unique, lofty character that had inspired this depth and fervor of friendship, or by the pathetic constancy and pure affection of the poor, desolate old man before me, who tried to conceal his tenderness and sense of irremediable loss by a show of gruffness and philosophy. He never speaks of Thoreau's death, but always "Thoreau's loss," or "when I lost Mr. Thoreau," or "when Mr. Thoreau went away from Concord"; nor would he confess that he missed him, for there was not a day, an hour, a moment, when he did not feel that his friend was still with him and had never left him. And yet a day or two after, when I sat with him in the sunlit wood, looking at the gorgeous blue and silver summer sky, he turned to me and said: "Just half the world died for me when I lost Mr. Thoreau. None of it looks the same as when I looked at it with him." He took me through the woods and pointed out to me every spot visited and described by his friend. Where the hut stood is a little pile of stones, and a sign, "Site of Thoreau's Hut," and a few steps beyond is the pond with thickly wooded shores,—everything exquisitely peaceful and beautiful in the afternoon light and not a sound to be heard except the crickets or the "z-ing" of the locusts which Thoreau had described. Farther on he pointed out to me, in the distant landscape a low roof, the only one visible, which was the roof of Thoreau's birthplace. He had been over there many times, he said, since he lost Mr. Thoreau, but had never gone in,—he was afraid it might look lonely! But he had often sat on a rock on front of the house and looked at it.[45]

Channing handed Emma Lazarus a farewell gift; when she opened the package, she found Thoreau's pocket compass and a copy of the Channing biography.[46]

In these years following Thoreau's death, Emerson found

that Channing's companionship still wore well. After the two had walked to "Becky Stow's Hole," Emerson commented in his journal on Nature's incessant gallop and whirl, and added: "And 'tis the same with my companion's genius. You must carry a stenographic press in your pocket to save his commentaries on things and men, or they are irrecoverable. I tormented my memory just now in vain to restore a witty criticism of his, yesterday, on a book." [47]

Nor did Channing ever weaken in respect and affection for the man who had been his unfailing champion from those first hopeful, golden years. He demanded that even the photographer do his friend justice. Occasionally he passed a night in Plymouth with the Marston Watsons, whose estate Hillside had been surveyed and landscaped by Thoreau. Invariably he turned to the wall a photograph of Emerson that hung in the guest room, because it was the worst likeness he had ever seen. [48]

In the 1870's Channing composed an imaginary dialogue entitled "Critics of Literature," in which the speakers were Emerson, Lowell, and himself. Here he caricatured certain opinions of his fellow critics, under the pretense that their tongues had been loosened by strong drink. Despite this element of fantasy, I believe that the bantering manner and the profusion of puns (most of them atrocious) are truer to the habitual give-and-take between Channing and Emerson than is the stilted dialogue of *Thoreau, the Poet-Naturalist*. "Critics of Literature" has, quite understandably, remained unpublished; but a sample here may be useful to suggest the evanescent word-play that was to Emerson one of the delights of Channing's conversation:

E. There are never more than a hundred persons whose opinions on literature are worth having, alive at the same moment.

C. I know Emerson that you have these exclusive views and that you write your books according to the same, whereby you do not sell more than a hundred copies of one of your editions. But for the mass, the reading public, the writer needs to consult his style, in short, to write down or up to the times. . . .

L. Pray, Mr. C, if you hold these opinions upon literature, why did you not accommodate your own productions to them, I will not call them verses because they turn slowly if they turn at all.

E. C. is a careless, slovenly writer. Here and there we catch a good line which shows the hand of the master, and then there are long deluges of carelessness.

C. I admire your frankness, Mr. Emerson, but the fact is I never published a careless line in my life, that is, so far as I know. You stole the above from that nincompoop F.B.S.,* who was born and bred a shoemaker and who has never forgotten his awl.

L. His all was deficient in point. . . .

E. Longfellow . . . is a careful writer and he has been very much read both here and in England, but it is my humble opinion that he never wrote a single line of poetry in his life that will last half a century.

C. Why, who does write verse to suit you?

E. I like some of your lines, C, pretty well, and there is one I have actually quoted,

<blockquote>If my bark sink etc.—†</blockquote>

Yes, I have cited it.

L. Out of mind, out of sight; as I never could read any of C's verses (as he calls them) I cannot of course recall that line and pray what does it mean.

E. Why its meaning is as plain as a pig in a poke. Its bark is worse than its bite, that's all. . . . I have always insisted upon it, L., that you were a good critic and yet you have your prejudices. You could never read anything of Thoreau's, so you say.

L. Did you ever, E.

* Franklin B. Sanborn.

† In this passage Channing misquotes himself. "If my bark sink" was "If my bark sinks" in the 1843 edition. But Emerson also dropped the *s* when he quoted this line in his essay on Montaigne.

E. No, I never did.

L. Well, how could you expect me to. I cared nothing for
T. personally as you did. He was a dull, dogmatic, quarrelsome
country man, and I am by nature a cit. I never could read a
line that he wrote any more than you.

E. But I know what is in his writings because he copies
them from mine.

C. Poor E., in vino veritas. Both he and L. must have had
two bottles of port apiece at the Atlantic Club.[49]

The "Critics" joined the pile of unpublished—and largely
unpublishable—manuscripts that grew steadily higher.
Though less hopeful of success than in his younger days,
Channing was now far more industrious. But he had not
renounced his walking habits wholly. Back in July of 1866,
he had climbed Monadnock with Emerson, Annie Keyes,
and a party of boys and girls from Concord (Tom Ward,
Eddie Emerson, Moorfield Storey, Una Hawthorne, Ellen
Emerson, and Lizzie Simmons). One night was drenching,
and the next was cold; but the charm of mists and rainbows,
and of songs around the campfire, was compensation
enough.[50] In the next ten years, Channing returned to the
mountain summer after summer, often on the fringes of a
youthful party. He would keep to himself; but it was com-
forting to have neighbors on that untamed peak, and to
receive their offering of food and drink.[51] On the occasions
when he camped quite alone, both the hardships and the
rewards were the greater. Afterwards, as he recalled these
expeditions, and saw himself crouching damply under a
leaky umbrella beneath a dripping roof of boughs, eating
biscuits from a bag, he wondered why he had invited such
discomfort. But already he had answered the question in
a notebook:

I have said nothing I think about the strange feeling I have
here alone; it is not solitude, but a kind of singular wonder

at being in the place by myself, after all the people have gone down the hill, a degree of stillness and beauty unlike all else I know. It affects the mind strangely. I cannot give it a name as yet, but it has a soft awe about it, a recognition of the greatness of the works of providence. It is novel and continues so. Our own species has lost its wonder for us, while nature is fresh and new.[52]

Now that his tramps in the woods were but occasional, he fell into a new routine. He left for Boston daily on the 8:12 train. Rain or shine, he plodded down the aisle with his bulging cotton umbrella, and took the last seat of the last car, to sit as far from people as he could.[53] Dozens of flimsy notebooks, with records of his readings, suggest that he did his business in the Boston Public Library and the Athenaeum. Usually he was back in Concord at supper time; but when he fed himself, it was a meager meal, for Channing was abstemious. For several years after his removal to Middle Street, he kept a housekeeper, an Irishwoman named Ann Carney; presumably she cooked the scant rations which he supplied. Sometimes the Emersons would send over some soup in a pail. Occasionally, when Channing was confined by illness, the two ladies who rented half of the house, Mrs. Wetherbee and Mrs. Newton, would make him eggnogs.[54]

His clothes grew ever shabbier. He had told Emerson in 1863:

that old age was cheap. Time drew out his teeth gratis, and a suction plate would last him as long as he lived; he did not go to the hairdresser, for Time cut off his hair; and he had lived so long, and bought so many clothes, that he should not need to buy any more.[55]

His house was a match for his clothing. He chinked the loose window frames and the keyholes with newspaper to keep out the wintry winds, and sometimes he plastered the panes with paper, too. One of his neighbors observed that this extra insulation was in order that he might smoke the same smoke twice over.[56]

Channing's daughter Margaret, who was then Mrs. Thacher Loring, kept herself informed through the housekeeper about his way of life. Hearing that he felt very poor, Margaret arranged to pay his milk bill regularly. One day she and her sister paid a surprise visit to the house in their father's absence, and found in the attic so many expensive books and so many playbills of recent performances in theater and opera, that their sympathy was severely tested. Channing, too, was troubled; he wrote his children forbidding them to enter his home. Yet Margaret continued to pay for milk.[57]

Once when Channing mentioned his loneliness to Mrs. Emerson, she told him it was his own fault; and for a brief time he even avoided her house.[58] But friendship quickly got the better of his petulance, and he continued to be a regular Sunday visitor.

To Emerson, he was one of the tangibles in a world that for the old philosopher was gradually dissolving in mist. When Channing called at the white house on the morning of April 27, 1882, his host remembered him and asked him to come to dinner again soon. That night Emerson died, and for Channing there ended the last relationship of intimacy and affection.

Within a few weeks, his isolation brought him nearly to his knees. He wrote a pleading letter to Margaret, in the care of Wentworth Higginson, whose home she had left some twenty years before. He begged her to take him under her roof. He almost took the blame for his unhappy state: he had been "forsaken by them who should be his succor and support because thro' his weakness and helplessness, he became and has so long remained separate from them." Enclosed with this plea was a similar one to Higginson, which seemed to assume that Margaret's roof was Higginson's also. Wentworth replied, offering sympathy only. He reminded Channing that the four oldest children were all married, with homes of their own, that their husbands and wives would be their natural counselors in this matter. If Margaret sent any direct reply, the letter is lost.[59]

Channing continued to read copiously, and to scratch away with his pen. He published two more volumes of verse: *Eliot* in 1885, and *John Brown and the Heroes of Harpers Ferry* in 1886. Neither affected his standing perceptibly as a man of letters. He compiled a "Manual of Words and Phrases (Chiefly English) in Great Part Recent or Obsolete," running to 382 manuscript pages and over 10,000 definitions; he copied it diligently in a crabbed hand, and bound the sheets with thread.

Mrs. Emerson still encouraged his visits, serving his supper every Sunday evening. On these occasions, he gave as well as received. Helen Legate, a young schoolteacher who boarded at the Emersons', found him invariably interesting. It seemed to her that he arrived each week with a subject of conversation well prepared, and this he pursued to the end. When interrupted, he was always courteous, and ready to answer questions, but at the earliest moment that politeness would allow, he returned to his subject.[60]

Although he continued his lonely life in Concord, his children watched him unobtrusively. Occasionally there were meetings; but these were dangerous, as the poet was unpredictable. When Caroline's son Chilton Cabot was engaged to be married, Caroline planned a surprise for her father. On a day when Channing was to stop in at the adjoining apartment for an eggnog, she and her prospective daughter-in-law sat with Mrs. Wetherbee and Mrs. Newton in their front parlor, waiting for the call. Channing knocked, and entered. Before anyone could speak, he retreated, out the front door and in his own half of the house. Caroline followed, and called, "Don't you know me, Father?" "Yes," he answered, "you're Itty Channing"; and he climbed the stairs without his eggnog.

After the Chilton Cabots had set up housekeeping in Concord, they, too, made friendly overtures, offering Channing a home with them. The reply was civil. Channing would be happy to accept, if they might arrange never to have visitors, and if all his meals might be served in his room.[61]

He continued in his own house.

"Come My Little Skipjack"
(1891–1901)

. . . Uncle Abel, often shall I see thy ghost and next
nature will come and set me on her thumb, come my
little skipjack, here is apoplexy or paralysis, (numb
palsy they call it in the country) or a fit, and crack—
I shall be even as Uncle Abel was: saved, if not worse.[1]

In the summer of 1891, Channing fell sick for several
weeks, and was the despair of Mrs. Wetherbee and Mrs.
Newton, his tenants, for they could neither take care of him
nor persuade him to hire a nurse. In this crisis, Frank Sanborn intervened and invited Channing to share the home
which the Sanborns had built eleven years before on the
bank of the Sudbury River. Mrs. Sanborn believed that the
house was none too large for their two boys and themselves;
but her husband overrode her veto, and on September 8
brought the sick poet home in a carriage.[2]

Channing was not a tractable patient. He promptly dis-
charged a nurse whom Sanborn had engaged; and when
Dr. Titcomb, upon examination, prescribed a bath, the poet

flatly refused to undergo such unfamiliar therapy. But the Doctor stood his ground. He called to Bill Tobin, a man-of-all-work who was helping the Sanborns; and while Dr. Titcomb held his patient, Bill undressed him. Then, together, they placed him in the bathtub. For serving as the Doctor's accomplice, Bill Tobin was rewarded by never again being employed at the Sanborns'.[3]

The outcome vindicated Dr. Titcomb, for Channing steadily gained strength. Sanborn himself acted as nurse, assisted by Mrs. Sanborn and a servant. As soon as the patient had recovered sufficiently, he authorized the sale of his house and the removal of his goods; Sanborn promptly saw to both transactions. In order that no harm should come to the objects most valued, Sanborn offered to move them all by hand; and Channing jotted down this memorandum as a guide:

Box of smoking tobacco (right of bookshelf); pipe on table. Umbrellas, canes; cases for umbrellas. Books under the bed in front lower room. Books on mantel, front room. American collection of woodcuts (or English). Same collection in part on bookshelves in living room. (Up one flight). Some in front upper room. Medical library (very valuable) under table in upper front room. Has Hippocrates in 7 volumes, Littre's edition; Copeland's Medical Dictionary, 3 vols Lizar's folio anatomic plates, and the like.

With the treasures specified Sanborn brought home five thousand other volumes.[4] To accommodate this library, he built shelves and cupboards in his west attic room with a special manuscript closet and a chimney safe. Also, to assure a habitable study for a poet and scholar, he constructed a hanging fireplace between the windows which overlooked the river.[5]

Happily, Mrs. Sanborn discovered that her permanent

guest was a man of courtesy and charm. He could still bark at others, but to her he was always gentle.[6] She was gratified also to receive considerable sums of money from him, even though her husband had made no financial arrangements with his boarder. Since Dr. Channing's death in 1876, Ellery had received a modest income from a trust fund. From this source, in the first five years of residence, Channing paid Mrs. Sanborn upwards of $2,000, at irregular intervals.[7]

Sanborn was grateful for Channing's board money and for his gentleness, but these were the lesser rewards of hospitality. In Channing and his manuscripts Sanborn saw a vein of mineral that, if properly and promptly worked, would yield a precious ore. First, there were the volumes of unpublished poetry, which needed only a discriminating editor —an editor who could trust his own judgment on variant readings, and who, in an emergency, could compose a brand-new line to clarify the meaning or to cure a lameness in the meter.* Secondly, there was a half century of Concord gossip in Channing's retentive head. Here was the single survivor of the Golden Age; and Sanborn, as the chronicler of that age, was quick to accept the responsibilities of manifest destiny.

Channing's bedroom was a pleasant northwest chamber directly below the attic study. Here, for his convenience, more bookshelves were installed, and for his comfort a Franklin stove, which provided not only heat but the cheer of an open hearth. Each night after supper, the men would light the stove and boil themselves a large pitcherful of water.

* Sanborn, writing to Higginson in 1902 about the forthcoming edition of Channing's poems, said: "When the text will give me variorum readings [I] take the best of the lot, or, sometimes, put in a better one. Mrs. Watson of Hillside, who has seen most of them, objects to any change; but Albee, like yourself, wants the text improved, at least by omissions." (Feb. 10, 1902; Massachusetts Historical Society)

Then they mixed their toddies; and as they sipped, Sanborn collected on his bold investment.[8]

On these evenings Channing traveled far into the past, describing his meeting with Abel Crawford at the Notch in 1836, and the appearance of the Bull's Head Tavern in Oak Park, Illinois, in 1840. He would recall his visit to Hawthorne in Salem in 1847, when he saw the house of the five gables on which his host was to make some literary alterations. He would relive the excursions to Walden and Fairhaven Bay, though he showed a peculiar reluctance to talk about Thoreau. He mentioned Emerson's dislike of Shelley and respect for Keats. At times Channing spoke consecutively and readily, hardly requiring a prod. At other times Sanborn had to question him; and often there were long periods of silence, except for the crackling in the iron fireplace.[9]

Despite this nightly exercise of memory, Channing had energy also for the present and shared the family life of the Sanborns and their guests. Other women than Mrs. Sanborn were impressed by his benevolence. Helen Legate, the young schoolteacher who as the Emersons' boarder had known him for several years, lived for a few months at the Sanborns' soon after Channing moved in. The poet immediately undertook to guide her reading. She appreciated this interest, although his well-meant attentions often took the forms of directive and of sarcasm. She read *The Egoist* at his suggestion because she did not dare refuse. He said he supposed she had read much of the Duchess's work; when she denied it, he remarked that this was at least *something* in her favor.[10]

To another young woman he was more gracious in manner,—even courtly and deferential. This was Mrs. Fiske Warren, in whom beauty and intellectuality were combined. Having studied at Oxford and traveled widely in Europe and the Orient, Mrs. Warren shared his interests in literature and the other arts and was his peer in all but age.* As a family friend of the Sanborns, she made occasional visits to Concord in the 1890's; and in 1897 and 1898 she and Channing exchanged letters frequently. He wrote to her effusively, thanking her for the loan of two volumes of Japanese prints, one of which he wanted back again, he had so enjoyed the study of it; philosophizing on time and immortality; advising her to read Thoreau if she wanted "real pabulum for the soul"; speculating on why Thoreau's handwriting so resembled Emerson's; bemoaning his own abandoned state—but not wholly abandoned either, since he enjoyed her faith and friendship. And in these screeds of misery and gratitude are flickerings of that seriocomic whimsy that the men of the Golden Age valued in their companion, as he declared himself then a "remainder-biscuit" and hack "not worth his purchase in discarded salt bags." [11]

The tenth anniversary of his removal to the Sanborns' came and went. Channing still puttered about his attic study, and sometimes wrote a scrap of verse; but his mind was hazy much of the time. Momentarily the fog would lift, and once more he would take Sanborn back on a reminiscent journey to Walden woods or the Illinois prairie. One day, when his mind was misty, he was visited by his grandson Chilton Cabot and his great-grandson Richard, five years old. Sitting in his study, his white hair crowned with a skullcap, he smiled kindly on the little boy, and looked like the most benign of Hebrew prophets. [12]

A few days before Christmas, 1901, he fell ill, and his death came quietly on the morning of December 23. At last his children might call on him without fear of rebuff. Except for the Sanborns, hardly a friend survived; but many

---

* Some years later, John Singer Sargent painted a portrait of Mrs. Warren and her daughter. The portrait supports the opinion of a contemporary that she was "the most beautiful, brilliant, soulful, and highly bred young matron anywhere in or about Boston."

of his neighbors had known him distantly, and to many others he was a legend of eccentricity and pathos. They came to the services at the Unitarian Church the day after Christmas: the duty-bound, the curious, the genuine mourners.

Frank Sanborn gave an address. Two men read from Channing's poems—including, no doubt, "If my bark sinks, 'tis to another sea." Among the six bearers were an Emerson, an Alcott, a Ricketson, and a Sanborn.

They buried him in Concord's Sleepy Hollow Cemetery, at one end of Author's Ridge, where the land begins to drop abruptly. Higher up are the graves of his close friends: Emersons, Thoreaus, Hawthornes, Alcotts. Channing is down there, somewhat off by himself, but a near neighbor to greatness.

The Curious Weave

(1817–1901)

Channing often used the imagery of weaving in his poetry. It is an appropriate figure for his own life, intricate mesh that it was of contradictions and complexities. Many of the threads in this curious weave have faded beyond detection, but four retain their identity and concern us now. It is for these that we keep his memory alive.

For almost sixty years, Channing was simultaneously a Concordian, a writer, an influence on other writers, and a practicing Transcendentalist. His significance would be less if he had been only two or three of these, instead of all four. These threads in the fabric of his life were woven together so tightly that, to follow any one of them, we must touch on them all. Yet each thread has its own color, and its course can be traced through the texture.

First, he was a villager of Concord, though less a villager than a saunterer on its outskirts. He was part of a vital social organism that throbbed excitedly. In the early 1840's, when he first arrived, the village was alive with "the Newness." Among its Concord apostles, only Emerson had as yet a real reputation; but the excitement was in the response to Emerson—and the respondents played a necessary part. Scores of young men were seeking out the philosopher. Hawthorne, at that time the master of the Manse, called them "hobgoblins of flesh and blood attracted hither by the wide-spreading influence of a great original thinker, who had his earthly abode at the opposite extremity of our village." [1] Channing was a hobgoblin. But in this relationship, Emerson gained as well as gave. We have seen the older man collecting Ellery's quips—those that he could bring to earth. It must have seemed to Emerson that it was much like catching butterflies in a net, and that, as with butterflies, the words were best when floating in their natural element. Yet he preserved many of them in his journals, thereby indicating why he found Channing companionable.

Even Hawthorne welcomed the newcomer, and was to remain his friend. "It might be that Ellery Channing came up the avenue to join me in a fishing excursion on the river. Strange and happy times were those when we cast aside all irksome forms and strait-laced habitudes, and delivered ourselves up to the free air, to live like the Indians or any less conventional race during one bright semicircle of the sun." [2] So with the other literary friendships. Channing knew Alcott from those earliest days, and was one of the first visitors to Fruitlands in the summer of 1843. Thoreau, too, was Ellery's friend from the first, though their close companionship was postponed by Henry's sojourn on Staten Island, and Channing's on Manhattan. It was Thoreau, of course, who negotiated the rental of the Red Lodge for the Channings.

The community was unique in the 1840's, and Channing helped to make it so. Half a century later, the old man with the cotton umbrella, hobbling to the station, was still making his contribution.

Channing published nine books and countless scraps of verse and prose. No single work is a masterpiece; in all his writings the faults snuggle too closely to the virtues. Thoreau called Channing's verse "sublimo-slipshod," [3] and this fairly reflects the contrasts within a single poem. The writer who produces a dozen immortal lyrics may be forgiven a hundred limping failures, but Channing's level soars and dips even in his most competent stanzas. This gives great difficulty to the editor, the anthologist, and the general reader.

His poems have value, however, beyond their undoubted biographical interest. When Channing's imagination ranges freely, it brings us memorable images and metaphors. Many of his lines and some of his stanzas achieve the melodies the poet heard in his inner ear. Perhaps the shorter lyrics are best, such as "The Gifts," "Life," "The Harbor," "Moonlight," and the longer but low-keyed "Wanderer." In such poems we are less frequently distracted by the archaic diction, awkward inversions, and padded lines, and consequently may enjoy their virtues of thought and statement. But students of nineteenth-century poetry know that many habits of phrase which now seem distortions were the conventional mannerisms of the period. Much that vexes us in Channing's verse is paralleled repeatedly in that of Emerson and Thoreau. One who has tuned his ear to Transcendental measures will be freer to receive what Channing expressed.

The prose works have differing values. Channing's most useful book, the biography of Thoreau, is a product of laborious amateur scholarship with a minimum of art, and may be best left to the scholars, who will continue to interpret Thoreau with its aid. *Conversations in Rome* is less readable today than in 1847; it still offers the drama and color of Italy, but the style is mannered and pretentious. Channing's best prose was written for the newspapers and for *The Dial*, including "The Youth of the Poet and Painter." He can still amuse us.

What of the "tracks in the snow" for others to walk in, which Channing felt was his only accomplishment?

Specific resemblances have already been noted between Channing's "Spider" and Emerson's "Humble-bee," and between "Hymn of the Earth" and "Brahma. If in these cases Emerson ever recognized any debt, the fact is unrecorded. Indeed, such indebtedness—if it existed at all—may have been wholly unconscious. In Channing's mind, however, these may have been among dozens of instances where a germ of an idea, or a well-turned phrase invented during a woodland walk, or a published poem, had been the seed from which another's work had flowered.

Furthermore, Channing's friends frequently incorporated his verses into their own texts without identifying the poet. No doubt they asked permission; but Channing at age fifty, with no literary success of his own, may well have rued this anonymity. Emerson had closed his essay on Montaigne with "If my bark sink, 'tis to another sea." In *A Week on the Concord and Merrimack Rivers* Thoreau had quoted Channing six times; in *Walden* four. Indeed, most of Thoreau's works may have seemed collaborations to his surviving friend. Not only had Channing's poems been adopted freely; he himself was often a character in the story. In *Walden* he makes several appearances, including this:

The one who came from farthest to my lodge, through deepest snows and most dismal tempests, was a poet. A farmer, a hunter, a soldier, a reporter, even a philosopher, may be daunted; but nothing can deter a poet, for he is actuated by pure love. Who can predict his comings and goings? His business calls him out at all hours, even when doctors sleep. We made that small house ring with boisterous mirth and resound with the murmur of much sober talk, making amends then to Walden vale for the long silences. Broadway was still and deserted in comparison. At suitable intervals there were regular salutes of laughter, which might have been referred indifferently to the last uttered or the forth-coming jest. We made many a "bran new" theory of life over a thin dish of gruel, which combined the advantages of conviviality with the clear-headedness which philosophy requires." [4]

In *Cape Cod* and *A Yankee in Canada* he was "my companion." It is understandable if in 1867, having recently completed the editing of one of these—and perhaps of both—Channing magnified his own obscurity, musing on his double role as the unknown character within the book and the unknown editor behind it.

Nearly a century later, we may see a significant relationship also to Whitman, to Dickinson, and to the twentieth-century poets. Here is not a progenitor, but a kind of uncle. As a Transcendentalist, he belonged to the first group that deliberately and boldly challenged the conventions of verse. It was Emerson who said, "It is not metres, but a metre-making argument that makes a poem," [5] thus pledging allegiance to substance as against form. But Emerson knew that, if the argument were to make meters, a poet must at least be present, as midwife if nothing more. Actually, we see all the Transcendental poets experimenting with technique, and often the irregularity of the rhythms and the obliquity of the rhymes seem intentional.

These poets, then—Channing among them—made tracks in the snow in a double sense. They issued hundreds of odd little verses—some jiggling, some sprawling, some raucous, some painfully pedestrian—and among them were numerous unconventional effects which later poets would imitate, or duplicate by accident. Of greater moment, the Transcendentalists, more than any other American poets, created a climate of freedom that made experimentation respectable.

Robert Frost would say later that writing free verse was like playing tennis with the net down. The Transcendentalists never got along without a net (nor, indeed, do the great writers of free verse). The Transcendentalists showed, however, that literary disciplines may be many and varied; and Channing, the least disciplined of all, made his modest gift to later generations by his membership in this rebellious fraternity.

These are the tracks in the snow that he least suspected.

Ironically, Channing was defeated by the Transcendentalism that had given meaning to his life.

It was his mistake to apply too literally the precepts of his master, Emerson. Not that Emerson had moulded Channing; long before their acquaintance began, the younger man was already the child of impulse that he remained to the end. But Emerson supplied the rationale that confirmed Channing in his pathetic course. When Channing was choosing mottoes for Thoreau's casket, he might have selected for his own the two familiar lines from "Self-Reliance": "A foolish consistency is the hobgoblin of little minds" and "I would write on the lintels of the doorpost, *Whim.*"

More than any other of the Transcendentalists, Channing lived for the moment. By normal standards, he lacked intellectual integrity. He was forever trying on new ideas, and casting them off—sometimes in the same poem. More often there were no ideas at all—only images. His notebooks are filled with concrete descriptions, but he seldom drew conclusions. The generalizations on men and nature that enrich the journals of Emerson and Thoreau are almost wholly absent from Channing's. Savoring the immediate present was to him the purest pleasure. In *Conversations in Rome* the Artist says, "During the first visit I made the Vatican, I scarcely looked at any thing; it was happiness to be surrounded with beautiful objects, beautifully placed, and looking from the balconies upon those beautiful landscapes is true enjoyment." [6] That was typical of the author, too.

This devotion to an hour-by-hour existence is tied to his

unwillingness to accept responsibility. Responsibility commits one's future hours; Channing would not make such bargains on his own. Yet if his nature, or the Voice Within, made commitments for him, that of course was beyond his control, and he bowed obediently.

Both his professional career as a poet and his domestic career as a husband and father illustrate this shelving of responsibility. It was Channing's belief, and his friends' also, that he was a poet of genius. In Transcendental language, it is the poet's genius that affords true perceptions. It is talent, that lesser faculty, that translates the experience of the poet into the experience of his reader. To Channing the problem was one of talent. It was still wrapped "in that tremendous napkin," as he said in 1867. Another sort of man would have gone to greater efforts to unwrap it, but Channing accepted the lack of talent as his fate. Perhaps Emerson's doctrine of the "metre-making argument" figured here also. This suggested an indifference to technique, according well with Channing's disorganized, undisciplined approach.

So with his marriage. It had been made in heaven, or by a divine alchemy that had united him to Ellen in spite of the protests of the prudent ones. Nature had commanded this; it was not his doing. Nor would he take responsibility for the children either; they too were gifts of nature. For a brief time, after Ellen took him back, he made an earnest effort to support his family; but the routines involved were against nature—his nature—and it was like swimming upstream.

Channing is a memorable figure in the story of our culture. His companionship enriched the lives of other, greater men. His poems have won a humble but permanent place in the anthologies. Some of his prose is highly useful to the scholars; some, particularly the zany portion, still offers entertainment. He contributed specifically to the writings of Emerson and Thoreau; as a "new poet" he helped prepare the way for newer and more talented successors whose voices, unlike his own, were worthy of their genius. Finally, his story demonstrates that devotedly following one's nature provides no guarantee of a serene and happy life. His career, both as poet and as husband, reminds us that Nature may beckon to tragic ends, as in other cases she steers one to triumph and glory.

Notes

In these notes, the authors of source material are designated by last names only except where clarity requires given names or initials. Occasionally a long title is abbreviated. The Bibliography includes full data.

For unpublished sources, the name of the library or private manuscript collection is given in parentheses. Thus a Fuller letter labeled (Houghton) is from the Fuller family collection in the Houghton Library. So likewise with Channing, Emerson, Higginson, Tappan, and Ward manuscripts in the Houghton Library. Material held by the Massachusetts Historical Society is labeled (M. H. S.).

Brackets have been used around dates which are not given in the source but may be assumed from internal evidence.

1. CHILDHOOD
(1817–1834)

1. Cunningham, *Owl's Nest*, 22.
2. Sanborn, "Ellery Channing on the Mystery of Shakespeare."
3. Barbara H. P. Channing to Margaret Curzon, Jan. 21, 1818; and Barbara H. P. Channing's diary, March, August, 1821. (M. H. S.)
4. Sanborn's Introduction to Channing, *Poems of Sixty-Five Years*, xiv.
5. E. W. Emerson, "John Murray Forbes," 383.
6. Forbes, *Letters and Recollections*, I, 44–45.
7. W. E. Channing, "Leviticus," Chap. IV. (Concord P. L.)

8. Cogswell, *Prospects of a School.* . . .
9. Sanborn, *Recollections*, II, 328–37.
10. Cogswell, *Life of J. G. Cogswell*, 156–57.
11. Forbes, *Letters and Recollections*, I, 44–45.
12. Channing, "Leviticus," Chap. IV. (Concord P. L.)
13. Woods, *Historical Sketches of Brookline, Mass.*, 190–91; and Poor, "Recollections of Brookline," 23.
14. Poor, "Recollections of Brookline," 23.
15. Pierce, *Memoir of Charles Sumner*, I, 85.
16. W. E. Channing, *Poems of Sixty-Five Years*, xiv–xv.
17. P. Holmes, *Tercentenary History of the Boston Public Latin School*, 102.
18. W. E. Channing, *Poems of Sixty-Five Years*, xiv.
19. Harvard College Admission Book.
20. For this and other details above, see Sanborn, "Ellery Channing on the Mystery of Shakespeare."

2. TRIFLECUT COLLEGE
(1834)

1. Sanborn, *Recollections*, II, 579.
2. Faculty Records, 1834, *passim*.
3. For a fuller account of the incident, see McGill, "Thoreau and College Discipline," *New England Quarterly*, XV (June, 1942), 349–53.
4. Harvard University Catalogue, 1834–35.
5. Harvard Term Book, 1st Term, 1834–35.
6. *Ibid.*
7. These excerpts are from Letters II and V of "The Youth of the Poet and Painter" in *The Dial*, Vol. IV, Nos. 1, 2 (July, October), 1843.

3. THE PROFESSIONAL POET
(1835–1839)

1. For Curzon's background, see letter of John P. Marquand to Keyes D. Metcalf, Nov. 7, 1949, affixed to index of Curzon family letters. (Houghton)
2. Town records, quoted by Joshua Coffin in *A Sketch of the History of Newbury*, 121.
3. Higginson to his mother, Mar. 5, 1847. (Houghton)

4. Curzon letters, 149.
5. Higginson to his mother, Mar. 5, 1847.
6. Caroline Sturgis to Margaret Fuller, Oct. 8, 1841. C. S. Tappan letters. (Houghton)
7. Curzon letters, 150.
8. *The Dial*, IV (July), 1843.
9. See Curzon letters of this year, particularly 312.
10. "On a Certain Man Who Came into Court on Wednesday, Sept. 23, 1835," Boston *Mercantile Journal*, Sept. 28, 1835.
11. Boston *Mercantile Journal*, May 20, 1835.
12. *Ibid.*, Apr. 22, 1835.
13. *Ibid.*, July 14, 1835.
14. *Ibid.*, Sept. 4, 1835.
15. *Ibid.*, Sept. 7, 1835.

4. LENOX AND THE WEST
(1839–1841)

1. James H. Perkins to his wife Sarah Elliott Perkins, June 4–10, 1838. (M. H. S.)
2. *Ibid.*
3. F. B. Sanborn, "Notes on William Ellery Channing."
4. Sanborn, *Recollections*, II, 574 ff.
5. Curzon letters, 456.
6. See correspondence of Caroline Sturgis (Tappan) in Houghton Library, particularly letters to Margaret Fuller, July 10, Sept. 9, 1841.
7. Curzon letters, 148. See also letter of John P. Marquand to Keyes D. Metcalf, Nov. 7, 1949, affixed to index of Curzon MSS. (Houghton)
8. Perkins to W. H. Channing, Mar. 18, 1838. (M. H. S.)
9. Perkins to his wife, May 29–June 2, 1838. (M. H. S.)
10. *The Dial*, IV (October), 1843.
11. Perkins to his wife, May 29–June 2, 1838.
12. Perkins to his wife, June 4–10, 1838.
13. Perkins to his wife, June 15–22, 1838.
14. Perkins to his wife, June 24, 1838.
15. Catherine M. Sedgwick II, Journal, Oct. 30, 1840. (M. H. S.)
16. *Ibid.*
17. Elizabeth D. Sedgwick to Charles Sedgwick, Mar. 16, 1838. (M. H. S.)

18. *Illinois in 1837,* 68.
19. Josiah Dwight to Catherine M. Sedgwick II, June 18, 1840. (M. H. S.)
20. F. B. Sanborn, "Ellery Channing on the Mystery of Shakespeare. With a Sketch of the Essayist." (Concord P. L.)
21. Register of Deeds of McHenry County, Woodstock, Ill.
22. *Illinois in 1837,* 70.
23. Josiah Dwight to Catherine M. Sedgwick II, June 18, 1840. (M. H. S.)
24. Sanborn, "Ellery Channing on the Mystery of Shakespeare." (Concord P. L.)
25. *Illinois in 1837,* 69.
26. Josiah Dwight to Catherine M. Sedgwick II, Nov. 8, 1840. (M. H. S.)
27. Sanborn, "Ellery Channing on the Mystery of Shakespeare." (Concord P. L.)
28. Josiah Dwight to Catherine M. Sedgwick II, Nov. 8, 1840. (M. H. S.)
29. Sanborn, *Recollections,* II, 573–74.
30. This entry, except for the April postscript, is dated Oct. 30, 1840.
31. Channing, *Leviticus,* Chap. V. (Concord P. L.)

5. TRANSCENDENTAL PEERAGE
(1839–1840)

1. Emerson to Ward, Oct. 3, 1839; Rusk.
2. Emerson to Channing, Jan. 30, 1840; Rusk.
3. Emerson to Margaret Fuller, Mar. 30, 1840; Rusk.
4. Emerson to Margaret Fuller, June 21, 1840; Rusk.
5. Emerson to Elizabeth Hoar, Sept. 12, 1840; Rusk.
6. Emerson to Caroline Sturgis, Sept. 13, 1840. Tappan letters. (Houghton)
7. *The Dial,* I, No. 2 (October, 1840).

6. ELLEN
(1840–1841)

1. Richard F. Fuller, *Recollections,* 15–16.
2. *Ibid.,* 18.
3. See Mrs. Fuller's voluminous correspondence with her children in the Fuller family letters. (Houghton)

4. Richard F. Fuller, *Recollections*, 41.
5. Mrs. Fuller to Arthur, Sept. 3, 1837. (Houghton)
6. Ellen to Richard, Nov. 15, 1840. (Houghton)
7. Mrs. Fuller to Margaret, Dec. 29, 1840; to Richard, Jan. 7, 1841. (Houghton)
8. Mrs. Fuller to Margaret, Jan. 20, 1841 (Houghton). The physician was Dr. Edward Jarvis (Johnston, *Memorial History of Louisville*, II, 253).
9. Mrs. Fuller to Arthur, Dec. 31, 1840. (Houghton)
10. Mrs. Fuller to Margaret, Feb. 14, 1841. (Houghton)
11. Mrs. Fuller to Margaret, Feb. 26, 1841. (Houghton)
12. Mrs. Fuller to Arthur, Mar. 8, 1841. (Houghton)
13. Ellen to Richard, Mar. 11, 1841. (Houghton)
14. Mrs. Fuller to Arthur, Apr. 3, 1841. (Houghton)
15. Mrs. Fuller to Margaret, Apr. 20, 1841. (Houghton)
16. Mrs. Fuller to Richard, May 5–6, 1841. (Houghton)
17. Mrs. Fuller to Margaret, June 6, 1841. (Houghton)
18. Quoted by Madeleine B. Stern in "Four Letters from George Keats," *PMLA*, LVI (March, 1941), 217–18.
19. Mrs. Fuller to Margaret, June 6, 1841. (Houghton)
20. Ellen to Richard, July 27–28, 1841. (Houghton)
21. *Ibid.*
22. Margaret to Mrs. Fuller, Aug. 5, 1841. (Houghton)
23. Charles E. Blackburn, "Some New Light on the *Western Messenger*," *American Literature*, XXVI (November, 1954), 325.
24. Much of the information on Perkins is drawn from *Owl's Nest* by Edith Perkins Cunningham.
25. From a letter of Feb. 12, 1840, to Mrs. James Freeman Clarke, quoted by Charles E. Blackburn, 336 n.
26. Sanborn, "William Ellery Channing and Daniel Ricketson," *New Bedford Mercury*, Centennial Number, Aug. 7, 1907.
27. Letter dated Apr. 5, 1841. (M. H. S.)
28. Barbara H. Channing to Mrs. W. W. Russel, Apr. 17, 1841. (M. H. S.)
29. Cist, *Cincinnati in 1841*, 116.
30. Perkins to W. H. Channing, Aug. 20, 1841. (M. H. S.)
31. Margaret to Mrs. Fuller, Aug. 31, 1841. (Houghton)
32. Ellery to Mrs. Fuller, Sept. 5, 1841. The italics are mine.
33. Ellery and Ellen to Margaret, Sept. 17, 1841. (Houghton)
34. Margaret to Ellery, Oct. 3, 1841. (Houghton)

35. Restored Marriage Record, Vol. IX, Probate Court, Hamilton Co., Ohio.
36. Perkins to W. H. Channing, Oct. 2, 1841. (M. H. S.)
37. Margaret to Mrs. Fuller, Oct. 5, 1841. (Houghton)

7. THE GOLDEN DAY
(1841–1844)

1. Sanborn, "The Friendships of Hawthorne," 183. Sanborn says that Channing met Hawthorne at Brook Farm.
2. Margaret to W. E. C., Oct. 3, 1841. (Houghton)
3. Mrs. Fuller to Margaret, Dec. 16, 1841. (Houghton)
4. Margaret to Richard, Nov. 17, 1841; and W. E. C. to Margaret, Mar. 20, 1842. (Houghton)
5. Mrs. Fuller to Richard, Jan. 6, 1842; Mrs. Fuller to Margaret, Jan. 2 and Apr. 5, 1842. (Houghton)
6. Margaret to Mrs. Fuller, Jan. 8, 1842. (Houghton)
7. Margaret to Mrs. Fuller, Feb. 5, 1842. (Houghton)
8. W. E. C. to Margaret, Mar. 20, 1842. (Houghton)
9. *Ibid.*
10. W. E. C. to Margaret, May 7, 1842. (Houghton)
11. W. E. C. and Ellen to Richard, Mar. 29, 1842. (Houghton)
12. Mrs. Fuller to Margaret, May 15, 1842. (Houghton)
13. W. E. C. and Ellen to Margaret, May 7, 1842. (Houghton)
14. Mrs. Fuller to Margaret, May 15, July 13, 1842. (Houghton)
15. Mrs. Fuller to Margaret, May 15, 1842. (Houghton)
16. Mrs. Fuller to Margaret, July 13, 1842. (Houghton)
17. Sanborn, "The Friendships of Hawthorne," 183.
18. Margaret to Richard, Aug. 5, 1842. (Houghton)
19. Hawthorne, *American Notebooks,* 145.
20. Elizabeth Hoar to Richard, Aug. 20, 1842. (Houghton)
21. Julian Hawthorne, *Hawthorne and His Wife,* I, 251–56.
22. Hawthorne, *American Notebooks,* 168, 317.
23. For Emerson's relations to Channing at this period, see Journal entry dated only "September," but probably 1842 (VI, 46–47); also entries of Aug. 20, Sept. 1, Oct. (?), 1842.
24. Emerson, Journal, Sept. 1, 1842.
25. Mrs. Fuller to Margaret, Aug. 30, 1842. (Houghton)
26. Hawthorne to Margaret Fuller, Feb. 1, 1843. (Houghton)
27. Emerson, Journal, Dec. 10, 1842.
28. *Ibid.,* Mar. (?), 1843 (VI, 357).

29. *Ibid.*
30. Hawthorne, *American Notebooks,* 175.
31. Thoreau to the Emersons, July 8, 1843; Harding.
32. W. E. C. to Margaret, May 21, 1843. (Houghton)
33. *Ibid.*
34. W. E. C. to Margaret, May 14, 1843. (Houghton)
35. Elizabeth Hoar to Richard F. Fuller, July 8, 1843. (Houghton)
36. *The Dial,* IV, No. 1 (July, 1843), 52.
37. Thoreau to Emerson, May 23, 1843; Harding.
38. Elizabeth Hoar to Richard F. Fuller, July 8, 1843. (Houghton)
39. *The Dial,* IV, No. 1 (July, 1843), 135.
40. W. E. C. to Margaret, May 14, 1843. (Houghton)
41. W. E. C. to Margaret, May 21, 1843. (Houghton)
42. W. E. C. to Margaret, June 19, 1843. (Houghton)
43. *Ibid.*
44. Emerson, MS Account Books, Feb. 6, 1844. (Houghton)
45. Arthur B. Fuller to Richard F. Fuller, July 30, 1843. (Houghton)
46. Emerson, MS Account Books, Oct. 17, 1843; Feb. 10, 1844. (Houghton)
47. W. E. C. to Richard F. Fuller, Aug. 2, 1843. (Houghton)
48. Caroline Sturgis to Emerson, Aug. 6, 15, 1843; Emerson to Caroline Sturgis, Aug. 20, 1843. (Houghton)
49. Caroline Sturgis to Margaret, July 10, 1841. (Houghton)
50. Caroline Sturgis to Margaret, Sept. 9, 1841. (Houghton)
51. Caroline Sturgis to Emerson, Oct. 16, 1841. (Houghton)
52. Caroline Sturgis to Emerson, Sept. 4, 1841. (Houghton)
53. Caroline Sturgis to Margaret, July 10, 1841. (Houghton)
54. Caroline Sturgis to Emerson, Feb. 4, 1845. (Houghton)
55. Woodberry, *Edgar Allan Poe,* 189.
56. Poe, *Complete Works,* IV, 174.
57. *Poems* (1843), 98.
58. *Ibid.,* 88.
59. Channing, Journal, July 19, 1852. (Houghton)
60. *The Dial,* IV (October, 1843), 181.
61. *Democratic Review,* XIII (Sept. 8, 1843), 309. See also Rusk, *The Letters of Ralph Waldo Emerson,* III, 193–98 and Note 331 for comment on this review and for excerpts from it.
62. W. E. C. to Mrs. Fuller, Thanksgiving Day, otherwise undated. Fuller Papers, XV, 135. (Houghton)
63. Margaret to Maria Rotch, Jan. 22, 1844. (Houghton)

64. From a copy made by Thomas Wentworth Higginson, dated March 3, 1844. (M. H. S.)
65. Mrs. Fuller to Barbara and Mary Channing, Apr. 21, 1844. (M. H. S.)

8. THE WANDERER
(1844–1847)

1. *Love Letters of Nathaniel Hawthorne*, II, 130.
2. *Ibid.*, II, 140.
3. Mrs. Fuller and Ellen to Margaret, June 15, 1844. (Houghton)
4. W. E. C. to Margaret, June 27, 1844. (Houghton)
5. Walter Harding, *The Days of Henry Thoreau*, 172.
6. Margaret to Arthur B. Fuller, July 3, 1844. (Houghton)
7. Margaret to Richard F. Fuller, Nov. 23, 1844.
8. Emerson to William Emerson, Dec. 3, 1844; Rusk.
9. Emerson to William Emerson, Apr. 5, 1845; Rusk.
10. See letters, above, to William Emerson; also one dated Dec. 31, 1844; Rusk.
11. W. E. C. to Emerson, Feb. 9, 1845; summarized in Rusk, III, 276.
12. W. E. C. to Richard F. Fuller, Feb. 21, 1845. (Houghton)
13. New York *Tribune*, Feb. 13, 1845.
14. *Ibid.*, Jan. 24, 1845.
15. Margaret to Richard F. Fuller, Mar. 2, 1845. (Houghton)
16. Emerson to William Emerson, Apr. 5, 1845; Rusk.
17. Emerson to S. G. Ward, Apr. 30, 1845. (Ward letters, Houghton)
18. Emerson to Anna Ward, Apr. 30, 1845. (Ward letters, Houghton)
19. Emerson to S. G. Ward, Apr. 30, 1845 (Ward letters, Houghton); also Middlesex Co. Reg. of Deeds, MS Vol. 472, pp. 434–35.
20. Arthur B. Fuller to Eugene Fuller, Sept. 3, 1845. (Houghton)
21. Higginson to his mother, Sept. 26, 1845. (Houghton)
22. Caroline Sturgis to Margaret, Thanksgiving Day, 1845. Fuller letters. (Houghton)
23. Mrs. Fuller to Richard, Feb. 10, 1846 (Houghton), and letter cited in Note 25.
24. See *Atlantic*, CXIV (September, 1914), 371.
25. Margaret to Richard F. Fuller, undated. (Houghton)
26. Emerson to S. G. Ward, Feb. 16, 1846; Rusk.
27. Margaret to Richard F. Fuller, undated. (Houghton)
28. Caroline Sturgis to Margaret, undated. Fuller letters. (Houghton)
29. Margaret to Richard F. Fuller, undated. (Houghton)

30. S. E. Morison, "Edward Channing, a Memoir," *Proceedings of the Massachusetts Historical Society,* LXVI (1942), 434–38.
31. "On Leaving Rome," *Woodman,* 1849.
32. New York *Evening Post,* Mar. 4–5, 1846.
33. Emerson to Caroline Sturgis, Aug. 3, 1846. Tappan letters. (Houghton)
34. Boston *Daily Evening Transcript,* July 3, 1846.
35. Emerson to Caroline Sturgis, Aug. 3, 1846. Tappan letters. (Houghton)
36. See Rusk's footnote, Emerson, *Letters,* III, 351.
37. Emerson, Journal, O, Flyleaf 3 [January, 1847]. (Houghton)
38. Emerson to Longfellow, Dec. 23, 1846, and footnote; Rusk.
39. Review of Emerson's, Channing's, and Story's poems. *Harbinger,* IV (Jan. 16, 23, 1847), 91–94, 106–9.
40. Emerson to James Munroe & Co., Jan. 1, 1847; Rusk.
41. F. Bowen, "Nine New Poets," *North American Review,* LXIV (April, 1847), 421.
42. *Literary World,* I, 23 (July 10, 1847), 542.
43. New York *Tribune,* July 1, 1847.
44. Emerson to George P. Bradford, June 29, 1847; Rusk.
45. *Conversations in Rome,* 18.
46. *Ibid.,* 79.
47. *Ibid.,* 111.
48. *Ibid.,* 19.
49. Emerson, Journal, CD, 137 [July, 1847]. (Houghton)
50. Carlyle, *Sartor Resartus,* Book II, Chap. 2, "Idyllic."
51. *Ibid.,* Book II, Chap. 9, "The Everlasting Yea."

9. NEAR HOME
(1847–1852)

1. From an interview with Mrs. Chilton Cabot of Concord, Dec. 30, 1932. The name of the little girl is lost.
2. This letter is undated, but internal evidence suggests January, 1851. In the Fuller collection it is XIV, 25. (Houghton)
3. Mrs. Fuller to Margaret, Feb. 21, 1847. (Houghton)
4. Mrs. Fuller to Margaret, May 21, 1849. (Houghton)
5. Emerson to Margaret, Apr. 11, 1850. Fuller letters. (Houghton)
6. Emerson, Journal, CO, 38 [May (?), 1851]. (Houghton)
7. Emerson to S. G. Ward, Dec. 2, 1844; Rusk.
8. Emerson, Journal, CO, 27 [May (?), 1851]. (Houghton)

9. Emerson, Journal, February, 1850.
10. Emerson, Journal, October, 1848. (Morgan)
11. Emerson, Journal, CO, 40 [May (?), 1851] (Houghton). An editor has written "(Sumner?)" in the MS.
12. Emerson, Journal, Oct. 24, 1850.
13. Emerson, Journal, October, 1848.
14. Emerson to Margaret, Aug. 29, 1847; Rusk.
15. Emerson, Journal, September, 1848.
16. Emerson, Journal, May, 1849.
17. For records of these sales, see Middlesex Co. Registry of Deeds, Vol. 564, pp. 461–63; Vol. 569, pp. 403–4.
18. Sanborn's typescript record of talks with W. E. C., September, 1901.
19. *Ibid.*
20. *Love Letters of Nathaniel Hawthorne*, II, 169.
21. *Ibid.*, II, 171.
22. Channing, Journal, May 8, 1852. (Houghton)
23. Mrs. Fuller to Margaret, Oct. 8, 1849. (Houghton)
24. Emerson, Account Books, July 30, 1850 (Houghton); also Emerson's letters written at this period to Horace Greeley, William Emerson, and Abby Larkin Adams; and on June 12, 1852, to Madame Arconati; Rusk. See also W. E. C. to Ellen, Aug. 3, 1850. Fuller letters. (Houghton)
25. Barbara Channing to Ellen, Aug. 23, 24, 1850. Fuller letters. (Houghton)
26. W. E. C. to Ellen, Aug. 3, 4, 1850. (Houghton)
27. William H. Fuller to Ellen, Aug. 15, 1851. (Houghton)
28. See the many references to the children's activities in the Fuller letters, September, 1851–January, 1852.
29. Mrs. Fuller to Ellen, Sept. 14, 1851. (Houghton)
30. Eugene Fuller to Richard F. Fuller, Sept. 14, 1851. (Houghton)
31. Mrs. Fuller to Richard, Oct. 19, Dec. 10, 1851; also William H. Fuller to Ellen, Nov. 2, 1851. (Houghton)
32. William H. Fuller to his mother, Dec. 28, 1851; Mrs. Fuller to Arthur, Jan. 25, 1852. (Houghton)
33. Mrs. Fuller to Ellen, Sept. 14, 1851. (Houghton)
34. W. E. C. to Ellen, Oct. 30, 1851. (M. H. S.)
35. Mary Channing Higginson to Ellen, Oct. 12, 1851. (M. H. S.)
36. W. E. C. to Ellen, Oct. 30, 1851. (M. H. S.)
37. Randall Stewart, *Nathaniel Hawthorne: A Biography*, Chap. VI.

10. CHANNING AND THOREAU
(1851–1853)

1. Thoreau, Journal, Nov. 9, 1851.
2. Emerson, Journal, June 13, 1852.
3. See Canby, *Thoreau*, 306.
4. Channing, Journal, June 17, 1853. (Houghton)
5. *Ibid.*
6. Channing, Journal, July 19, 1852. (Houghton)
7. *Ibid.*, May 14, 1852.
8. *Ibid.*, Sept. 9, 1852.
9. *Ibid.*, June 1, 1852.
10. *Ibid.*, May 14, 1852.
11. Thoreau, Journal, Nov. 9, 1851.
12. Channing, Journal, Dec. 31, 1852. (Houghton)
13. *Ibid.*, Aug. 12, 1852.
14. Channng, Journal, Dec. 16, 17, 18, 1852. (Houghton)
15. Thoreau, Journal, Mar. 20, 1858; Jan. 9, 1859; Dec. 8, 1859; Mar. 24, 1859.
16. Channing, Journal, June 1, 25, 1852. (Houghton)
17. *Ibid.*, July 25, 1852.
18. *Ibid.*, Jan. 9, 1853.
19. *Ibid.*, Apr. 10, 1853.
20. Emerson to Thoreau, Feb. 6, 1850; Rusk.
21. Mrs. Fuller to Arthur B. Fuller, Jan. 25, 1852. (Houghton)
22. T. W. Higginson to Ellen, Feb. 13, 1852. (M. H. S.)
23. Mrs. Fuller to Richard F. Fuller, Feb. 1, 1852. (Houghton)
24. Thoreau, Journal, Jan. 30, 1852.
25. *Ibid.*, Jan. 30, 1852.
26. Mrs. Fuller to Arthur, Mar. 9, 1852 (Houghton). This sermon was on March 7. Channing preached again in Plymouth on May 16. See his journal for that day.
27. Channing, Journal, May 2, 1852. (Houghton)
28. T. W. Higginson to (?), Nov. 19, 1852 (Houghton). The unnamed friend was probably Emerson.
29. Channing, Journal, Feb. 25, 1867. (Houghton)
30. Canby, *Thoreau*, 310–11.
31. Thoreau to Emerson, Feb. 23, 1848; Harding.
32. Thoreau, Journal, Mar. 12, 1854.
33. *Ibid.*, Apr. 22, 1852.
34. *Ibid.*, Jan. 30, 1852.

35. Channing, Journal, June 19, 1852. (Houghton)
36. Thoreau, Journal, May 25, 1853.
37. *Ibid.*, (?), 1841.
38. Channing, Journal, Apr. 17, 1853. (Houghton)

11. YEAR OF ESCAPE
(1853)

1. Channing, Journal, Apr. 9, 1853. (Houghton)
2. *Ibid.*, Feb. 20, 1853.
3. *Ibid.*
4. Richard F. Fuller to T. W. Higginson, Dec. 15, 1853. (M. H. S.)
5. Quotations in this and the two preceding paragraphs are from Channing, Journal, Apr. 17, 1853. (Houghton)
6. *Ibid.*
7. Channing, Journal, Apr. 19, 1853. (Houghton)
8. *Ibid.*
9. Channing, Journal, Apr. 20, 21, 1853. (Houghton)
10. *Ibid.*, Apr. 21, 23, 1853.
11. *Ibid.*, Apr. 23, 1853.
12. Mrs. Fuller to Ellen, May 1, 1853. (Houghton)
13. T. W. Higginson, memo, Nov. 14, 1853. (M. H. S.)
14. Mrs. Fuller to Richard, July 7, 1853. (Houghton)
15. T. W. Higginson, record of depositions. (M. H. S.)
16. Channing, Journal, May 25, 28, 1853. (Houghton)
17. *Ibid.*, May 9, 24, 1853.
18. See MS of Emerson's "Conversations with Henry D. Thoreau and Ellery Channing" in the Morgan Library; also Channing's *Thoreau, the Poet-Naturalist*, Chaps. 8, 9, which include many of these "conversations." The evolution of this material is discussed by F. B. Sanborn in his edition of *Thoreau, the Poet-Naturalist* (Boston, 1902) on pp. ix, 132, 133.
    See also Rollo G. Silver, "Ellery Channing's Collaboration with Emerson," *American Literature*, VII (March, 1935), 84–86; also Walter Harding, "Two F. B. Sanborn Letters," *American Literature*, XXV (May, 1953), 230–34.
19. Alcott, Journal, July 1, 1853.
20. Channing, Journal, June 26, 1853. (Houghton)
21. *Ibid.*, July 9, 1853.
22. Mary and T. W. Higginson to Ellen, July 12, 1853. (M. H. S.)
23. Channing, Journal, July 24, 1853. (Houghton)

24. Dr. Walter Channing to W. E. C., Dec. 13, 1853; T. W. Higginson to Judge Charles Allen, Dec. 15, 1853. (Copies in M. H. S.)
25. W. E. C. to S. G. Ward, May 20, 1853. Ward letters. (Houghton)
26. Channing, Journal, June 21, 1853. (Houghton)
27. Alcott, Journal, July 1, 1853.
28. Channing, Journal, July 24, 1853. (Houghton)
29. Ellen to Higginson, Oct. 4, [Nov. 11], 1853. (M. H. S.)
30. Dr. Walter Channing to Mary Higginson, Oct. 4, [Oct. 5], 1853. (M. H. S.)
31. These tragic events preceding the separation are reconstructed principally from Ellen's letters to Higginson of Oct. 4 and [Nov. 11].
32. T. W. Higginson to Mrs. Fuller, Nov. 18, 1853. (M. H. S.)
33. T. W. Higginson to Dr. Walter Channing, Nov. 18, 1853. (M. H. S.)
34. (M. H. S.)
35. Channing, Journal, Dec. 28, 1853. (Houghton)
36. *Ibid.*, Dec. 29, 1853.

12. THE INNER VOICE
(1853–1855)

1. See memoranda of Higginson recapitulating the events of the separation in Massachusetts Historical Society; also Mary Higginson to Ellen Fuller Channing, Sept. 26, 1853 (M. H. S.); Dr. Walter Channing to Mary Higginson, Oct. [3], 4, 1853; also, in Fuller letters, Ellen to Richard, Sept. 26, 1853 (Houghton).
2. Ellen to Richard, [Oct. 4], 1853 (Houghton). Also Ellen to Higginson, Oct. 4, [Nov. 11], 1853; Dr. Walter Channing to Mary Higginson, [Oct. 5], 1853. (M. H. S.)
3. Ellen to Higginson, [Nov. 11], 1853. (M. H. S.)
4. Higginson memo, [Nov.] 14, 1853. (M. H. S.)
5. Mrs. John Farrar, Dec. 8, 1853. (Houghton)
6. Ellen to Higginson, Feb. 4, 1855. (M. H. S.)
7. Mrs. Fuller to Ellen, [Nov. 27], 1853. (Houghton)
8. Rev. Barzillai Frost to Higginson, Nov. 30, 1853. (M. H. S.)
9. Higginson to Mary Higginson, [Nov. 15], 1853; Higginson to Dr. Walter Channing, Nov. 18, 1853; Dr. Walter Channing to Ellen, Nov. 27, 1853. (M. H. S.)
10. W. E. C. to Ellen, Nov. 25, 1853. (M. H. S.)

11. G. M. Brooks to Ellen, Dec. 8, 1853. (M. H. S.)
12. Ellen to W. E. C., Dec. 4, 1853. (Copy in M. H. S.)
13. Richard F. Fuller to Higginson, Nov. 30, Dec. 10, Dec. 14, 1853 (M. H. S.); also Higginson to Charles Allen, Dec. 15, 1853 (Copy in M. H. S.).
14. Dr. Walter Channing to George M. Brooks, Dec. 13, 1853. (Copy in M. H. S.)
15. Higginson memo, undated. (M. H. S.)
16. Richard F. Fuller to Higginson, [Dec. 15], 1853. (M. H. S.)
17. Ellen to W. E. C., Dec. 4, 1853. (Copy in M. H. S.)
18. Mrs. Fuller to Ellen, Nov. 27, 1853; Elizabeth Hoar to Ellen, Nov. 24, 1853; Mrs. John Farrar to Ellen, Dec. 8, 1853 (Houghton); also Rev. Barzillai Frost to Higginson, Nov. 30, 1853 (M. H. S.).
19. Frost to Higginson, Dec. 9, 1853; and telegram, E. Wild to Higginson, Dec. 21, 1853 (M. H. S.).
20. Miss M. A. Ripley to Ellen, undated. (Houghton)
21. Another letter from Miss Ripley to Ellen, undated. (Houghton)
22. Mrs. John Farrar to Ellen, Mar. 28, 1854; Frances Fuller to Ellen, Apr. 16, 1854 (Houghton). Also Ellen to Higginson, May 7, 1854; Ellen to Mary Higginson, June 25, 1854; Mary Higginson to her husband, June 30, 1854 (M. H. S.).
23. William H. Fuller to his mother, Jan. 12, 1854. (Houghton)
24. Ellen to Higginson, June 13, 1854; Ellen to Higginson, July 11, 1854; Higginson to Ellen, July 14, 1854. (M. H. S.)
25. Ellen to Higginson, July 11, 1854. (M. H. S.)
26. Ellen to Higginson, [Sept. 24, 1854]. (M. H. S.)
27. Ellen to Higginson, Aug. 11, 1854; Sept. 9, 1854. (M. H. S.)
28. Ellen and Marnie Channing to the Higginsons, Dec. 24, 1854. (M. H. S.)
29. Ellen to Higginson, [July 23], 1855. (M. H. S.)
30. Mrs. Fuller to the Higginsons, July 24, 1855. (M. H. S.)
31. Ellen to the Higginsons, [Aug. 13, 1855]. (M. H. S.)
32. Arthur B. Fuller to Eugene Fuller, Aug. 9, 1855. (Houghton)
33. Frances Fuller to Ellen, undated. (Houghton)
34. Arthur B. Fuller to Eugene Fuller, Aug. 9, 1855. (Houghton)
35. Ellen to Higginson, [Sept. 18, 1855]. (M. H. S.)
36. Higginson to Ellen, Sept. 21, 1855. (M. H. S.)
37. See draft of letter dated Sept. 21 which Higginson never sent. In this he recalls his earlier remarks. (M. H. S.)

38. W. E. C. to Higginson, Sept. 6 and [Sept. 25], 1855. (M. H. S.)
39. Higginson to Ellen, Oct. 23, 1855. (M. H. S.)

13. REDEMPTION
(1855–1856)

1. Arthur B. Fuller to Eugene Fuller, Oct. 15, 1855. (Houghton)
2. W. E. C. to Franklin B. Sanborn, [Oct. 26], 1855 (Concord P. L.). Channing dated this letter Feb. 26, 1855, an obvious error. The postmark is Oct. 29.
3. Ellen to Richard, Jan. 27, 1856. (Houghton)
4. For the correspondence between Ricketson and Thoreau, from which this account of their friendship—and of Channing's visit—is drawn, see Anna and Walton Ricketson, *Daniel Ricketson and His Friends*, 3–60, *passim*.
5. *Daily Mercury*, Aug. 27, 1856.
6. *Ibid.*, Nov. 4, 1856.
7. Higginson to Richard F. Fuller, Nov. 29, 1856. (Copy in M. H. S.)
8. Mrs. Fuller to Arthur, June 25, 1856. (Houghton)
9. Mrs. Fuller to Higginson, July (?), 1856 (M. H. S.)
10. Ellen to the Higginsons, Aug. 16, 1856. (M. H. S.); also Ellen to Richard, Aug. 16 and Sept. 15, 1856; Arthur to Eugene, Sept. 12, 1856; Mrs. Fuller to Richard, Sept. 9, 1856; Mrs. Fuller to Arthur, Sept. 9, 1956; Mrs. Fuller to Ellen, Sept. 15, 1856 (Houghton).
11. Higginson to Richard F. Fuller, Nov. 18, 1856. (Copy in M. H. S.)

14. THE LONELY ROAD
(1856–1891)

1. S. L. Morison, *By Land and by Sea*, 301–2.
2. A. and W. Ricketson, *Daniel Ricketson and His Friends*, 205.
3. Thoreau to H. G. O. Blake, Apr. 17, 1857; Harding. Also entries for April, 1857 in Channing's journal. (Houghton)
4. Emerson, Journal, July 26, Aug. 2, 1857. Also Thoreau, Journal, Aug. 22, Sept. 6, Sept. 18, 1857, and Thoreau to Ricketson, Aug. 18, 1857; Harding.
5. Ricketson, *op. cit.*, 149, 152–53; Boston *Sunday Globe*, Feb. 23, 1930.
6. Ricketson, 78.
7. *Ibid.*, 81–83, 309; Thoreau, Journal, Nov. 30, 1858.

8. This letter, dated Jan. 18 [1858], is in the Massachusetts Historical Society collection.
9. Sanborn, *Recollections*, II, 398.
10. Thoreau to Ricketson, Oct. 31, 1858; Harding.
11. Thoreau to Blake, Nov. 4, 1860; Harding. Also Thoreau, Journal, Aug. 4–9, 1860, and Channing's "Monadnoc" Journal (Houghton).
12. Sanborn, *Life of Henry David Thoreau*, 368–69.
13. Thoreau to Ricketson, Mar. 22, 1861; Harding.
14. A. and W. Ricketson, *Daniel Ricketson and His Friends*, 312–13, 320.
15. Sanborn, *Recollections*, II, 394 ff.
16. Canby, *Thoreau*, 438.
17. Alcott, Journal, May 6, 1862.
18. So reported in the Boston *Evening Transcript*, May 10, 1862.
19. Quotation unidentified.
20. William Browne, "The Shepherd's Pipe," Eclogue IV, line 170.
21. John Gower, Prologue to *Confessio Amantis*, lines 58–60.
22. See Frances H. Allen, *Thoreau's Editors*, 7–8.
23. Canby, *Thoreau*, 441; Sanborn, *Recollections*, II, 394–97.
24. Allen, 10–11.
25. Ricketson, 155.
26. Alcott, Journal, July 19, 1871.
27. See Sanborn's introduction, pp. x–xi, to his edition of *Thoreau, the Poet-Naturalist*, 1902; also Harding, *A Thoreau Handbook*, 16.
28. Channing, Journal, Mar. 5, 1867. (Houghton)
29. Recalled by Mrs. Chilton Cabot, Dec. 30, 1932.
30. Canby, *Thoreau*, 68.
31. Channing, Journal, Apr. 22, 1867. (Houghton)
32. *Ibid.*, Feb. 26, 1867.
33. *Ibid.*
34. *Ibid.*
35. *Ibid.*, Feb. 27, 1867.
36. *The Wanderer*, 28–29.
37. Emerson to Edward Waldo Emerson, Dec. 17 and [c. 18], 1871; Rusk.
38. See Sanborn's introduction to his edition of *Thoreau, the Poet-Naturalist*, x–xi.
39. *Ibid.*, xi–xii.
40. *Ibid.*, xii–xiii.
41. *Ibid.*, xiii.

42. For an account of the Emersons' Thanksgivings, see Rusk's footnote in *Letters*, VI, 315.
43. See Rusk's footnote in *Letters*, V, 382.
44. Emerson to Ellen Emerson, Oct. 19, 1871.
45. Emma Lazarus, *Poems*, I, 12–14. In a biographical introduction, the editor quotes much of the journal; at times she paraphrases. The long excerpt is a direct quotation.
46. *Ibid.*
47. Emerson, Journal, Sept. 24, 1864.
48. T. R. Ybarra, *Young Man of Caracas*, 233–34.
49. "Critics of Literature," in volume with title page: "Eliot and John Brown in this volume/After 1870."
50. Emerson, Journal, July 2, 1866.
51. Recalled by Judge Prescott Keyes in an interview, Sept. 2, 1936.
52. Channing, "Monadnoc" Journal, Aug. 11, 1870. (Houghton)
53. From interviews with Mrs. Chilton Cabot (Dec. 30, 1932) and Miss Helen A. Legate (Sept. 2, 1936).
54. Recalled by Mrs. Cabot (Dec. 30, 1932).
55. Emerson, Journal, Nov. (?), 1863.
56. Recalled by Judge Prescott Keyes, Sept. 2, 1936.
57. T. W. Higginson memo regarding W. E. C., June, 1882. (M. H. S.)
58. Rusk, *Life of Ralph Waldo Emerson*, 508.
59. These letters are in the Massachusetts Historical Society collection.
60. Recalled by Miss Helen A. Legate, Sept. 2, 1936.
61. Both incidents recalled by Mrs. Chilton Cabot, Dec. 30, 1932.

15. "COME MY LITTLE SKIPJACK"
(1891–1901)

1. Channing, Journal, Apr. 22, 1867. (Houghton)
2. Some details are from Sanborn's typescript account in the Concord Public Library; others were supplied by Mr. Francis Sanborn, Feb. 1, 1952.
3. Recalled by Judge Prescott Keyes, Sept. 2, 1936.
4. Sanborn, "Dates and Circumstances. . . ." (Concord P. L.)
5. Recalled by Mrs. Herbert Hosmer, Sept. 2, 1936.
6. Recalled by Mr. Francis Sanborn, Feb. 1, 1952.
7. Sanborn, "Dates and Circumstances. . . ." (Concord P. L.)
8. Recalled by Mr. Francis Sanborn, Feb. 1, 1952.

9. See Sanborn's typescript record in Concord P. L. of talks with W. E. C.; also random references in his several biographical sketches of Channing, and in *Recollections*.
10. Recalled by Miss Helen Legate, Sept. 2, 1936.
11. Channing, autograph letters. (M. H. S.)
12. Recalled by Mrs. Chilton Cabot, Dec. 30, 1932.

16. THE CURIOUS WEAVE
(1817–1901)

1. Hawthorne, *Works,* II, 41.
2. *Ibid.,* II, 31–32.
3. Thoreau, Journal, III, 118.
4. Thoreau, *Walden,* 414–15.
5. Emerson, *Complete Works,* III, 9.
6. Channing, *Conversations in Rome,* 16.

Bibliography

UNPUBLISHED SOURCES

Libraries and private collections are given in parentheses.

Channing, Barbara H. P. Diary. (Massachusetts Historical Society)
———. Letters. (Mass. Hist. Soc.)
Channing, Walter. "List of Midwifery Cases from 1811." (Mass. Hist. Soc.)
Channing, William Ellery II. "Critics of Literature," in MS volume with title page: "Eliot and John Brown in this volume/After 1870." (Concord P. L.)
———. Journals. Five notebooks covering years 1852–64. (Houghton)
———. Journal, 1867. Included in same volume are MS poems with miscellaneous notes. (Houghton)
———. "Journal and Pencillings on Monadnoc," 1869, 1870, 1871, 1875, 1876. (Houghton)
———. Letters. (Mass. Hist. Soc.)
———. "Leviticus." Edited and published in part by Francis B. Dedmond. (Concord P. L.) See "Dedmond" under Published Sources.
Curzon family papers. (Houghton)
Dwight, Josiah. Letters. (Mass. Hist. Soc.)
Emerson, Ralph Waldo. Account books. (Houghton)
———. "Conversations with Henry D. Thoreau and Ellery Channing." (Morgan)
———. Journals. (Houghton, Morgan)

Fuller family papers. (Houghton)

Harvard College Admission Book. (Harvard Univ. Archives)

Harvard College Records/Acts of the Corporation. Vol. VII (April 12, 1827–September 15, 1836). (Harvard Univ. Archives)

Harvard Faculty Records, 1834. (Harvard Univ. Archives)

Harvard Term Books. First Term, 1834–35 (September 1–November 30, 1834). Also 1837–39, *passim.* (Harvard Univ. Archives)

Hawthorne, Nathaniel. Letters to Evert A. Duyckinck, March 13, 20, 1847. (New York P. L.)

Higginson, Thomas Wentworth. Letters. (Houghton)

———. Letters and memoranda. (Mass. Hist. Soc.)

Perkins, James Handasyd. Letters. (Mass. Hist. Soc.)

Records of the Boston Athenaeum. Vol. I (1827–35) and Vol. II (1835–43).

Records of the First Unitarian Church of Cincinnati, Ohio.

Register of Deeds, McHenry Co., Ill.

Registry of Deeds, Middlesex Co., Mass.

Restored Marriage Record. Vol. IX, Probate Court, Hamilton Co., Ohio.

Sanborn, Franklin B. "Dates and circumstances in regard to the coming of W. E. Channing to live with F. B. Sanborn." (Concord P. L.)

———. "Ellery Channing on the Mystery of Shakespeare. With a Sketch of the Essayist." (Concord P. L.)

———. "Notes on William Ellery Channing, August 28, 1901 to September 17, 1901." (Concord P. L.)

———. "Was Ellery Channing a Knave?" (Concord P. L.)

Sedgwick, Catherine M. II. Journal. (Mass. Hist. Soc.)

Sedgwick family letters. (Mass. Hist. Soc.)

Thoreau, Henry D. Journals. (Morgan)

Tappan, Caroline Sturgis. Letters. (Houghton)

Ward, Samuel Gray. Letters. (Houghton)

Williams, Paul O. "The Transcendental Movement in American Poetry," unpublished dissertation, Univ. of Pennsylvania, 1962.

PUBLISHED SOURCES

Alcott, A. Bronson. *The Journals of Bronson Alcott,* ed. Odell Shepard. Boston: Little, Brown, 1938.

Allen, Francis H. *Thoreau's Editors. History and Reminiscence.* Chapel Hill: The Thoreau Society, 1950.

Barrows, Chester L. *William A. Evarts.* Chapel Hill: Univ. of North Carolina Press, 1941.

Bartol, C. A. General review, *Christian Examiner,* XLII (March, 1847), 254–55.

Blackburn, Charles E. "Some New Light on the *Western Messenger*," *American Literature,* XXVI (November, 1954), 325 ff.

Boston *Daily Evening Transcript,* July 3, 1846.

Boston *Mercantile Journal,* 1935–39.

Bowen, Francis. "Nine New Poets," *North American Review,* LXIV (April, 1847), 402–34.

Canby, Henry S. *Thoreau.* Boston: Houghton Mifflin, 1939.

Channing, William Ellery II. *Conversations in Rome between an Artist, a Catholic, and a Critic.* Boston: Crosby & Nichols, 1847.

———. *Eliot. A Poem.* Boston: Cupples, Upham, 1885.

———. *John Brown, and the Heroes of Harpers Ferry. A Poem.* Boston: Cupples, Upham, 1886.

———. *Near Home.* Boston: James Munroe, 1858.

———. *Poems.* Boston: Little, Brown, 1843.

———. *Poems: Second Series.* Boston: James Munroe, 1847.

———. *Poems of Sixty-Five Years,* ed. Franklin B. Sanborn. Philadelphia and Concord: James H. Bentley, 1902.

———. *Thoreau, the Poet-Naturalist.* Boston: Roberts Brothers, 1873.

———. *Thoreau, the Poet-Naturalist,* ed. Franklin B. Sanborn. With Memorial Verses. Boston: Charles E. Goodspeed, 1902.

———. *The Wanderer.* Boston: J. R. Osgood, 1871.

———. *The Woodman, and Other Poems.* Boston: James Munroe, 1849.

———. "The Youth of the Poet and Painter," *The Dial,* IV (1843–44), 48–58, 174–86, 273–84, 427–54.

Cist, Charles. *Cincinnati in 1841.* Cincinnati: Printed and published for the author, 1841.

Clarke, James Freeman. *Autobiography, Diary, and Correspondence,* ed. E. E. Hale. Boston: Houghton Mifflin, 1891.

Coffin, Joshua. *A Sketch of the History of Newbury, Newburyport and West Newbury, from 1635 to 1845.* Boston: S. G. Drake, 1845.

Cogswell, Joseph G. *The Life of Joseph Green Cogswell.* Cambridge: Privately printed, 1874.

———. Prospectus of a School to Be Established at Round Hill. . . . Cambridge: Hilliard & Metcalf, 1823.

Cunningham, E. P. *Owl's Nest.* Cambridge: Printed for private distribution, 1907.

Dedmond, Francis B. "William Ellery Channing on Thoreau: An Unpublished Satire," *Modern Language Notes,* LXVII (January, 1952), 50–52.

Dwight, John S. Review of *Poems: Second Series, Harbinger,* IV (January 16, 1847), 91–94; IV (January 23, 1847), 106–9.

———. Review of *Conversations in Rome, Harbinger,* V (July 10, 1847), 69–71.

Emerson, Edward Waldo. "John Murray Forbes," *Atlantic,* LXXXIV (September, 1899), 382–96.

Emerson, Ralph Waldo. *The Letters of Ralph Waldo Emerson,* ed. R. L. Rusk. 6 vols. New York: Columbia Univ. Press, 1939.

———. *The Journals of Ralph Waldo Emerson,* ed. E. W. Emerson and W. E. Forbes. 10 vols. Boston and New York: Houghton Mifflin, 1909–14.

———. "Mr. Channing's Poems," *The United States Magazine and Democratic Review,* XIII (September, 1843), 309–14.

———. "New Poetry," *The Dial,* I (October, 1840), 2.

———. Review of *Poems* by William Ellery Channing, *The Dial,* IV (July, 1843), 135.

———. *The Complete Works of Ralph Waldo Emerson,* ed. E. W. Emerson, 12 vols. Boston: Houghton Mifflin, 1903–4.

Forbes, John Murray. *Letters and Recollections,* ed. Sarah Forbes Hughes. Boston: Houghton Mifflin, 1899.

Fuller, Richard F. *Recollections of Richard F. Fuller.* Boston: Privately printed, 1936.

Gilman, Caroline, ed. *The Sybil, or New Oracles from the Poets.* New York: Wiley & Putnam, 1847.

Harding, Walter. *The Days of Henry Thoreau.* New York: Knopf, 1965.

———. *A Thoreau Handbook.* New York: New York Univ. Press, 1959.

Harvard College Catalogue, 1834–35.

Hawthorne, Julian. "Hawthorne's Last Years," *Hawthorne Centenary Celebration at The Wayside, July 4–7, 1904.* Boston: Houghton Mifflin, 1905.

———. *Nathaniel Hawthorne and His Wife.* Boston: Houghton Mifflin, 1884.

Hawthorne, Nathaniel. *American Notebooks,* ed. Randall Stewart. New Haven: Yale Univ. Press, 1932.

———. *Love Letters of Nathaniel Hawthorne.* 2 vols. Chicago: Privately printed, The Society of Dofobs, 1907.

———. Review of *Conversations in Rome, Literary World,* I (July 10, 1847), 542.

———. Review of *Conversations in Rome,* New York *Tribune,* July 1, 1847.

———. *Works.* 12 vols. Boston: Houghton Mifflin, 1883.

Holmes, Oliver Wendell. *A Memoir of Henry Jacob Bigelow.* Cambridge: J. Wilson, 1891.

Holmes, Pauline. *Tercentenary History of the Boston Public Latin School, 1635–1935.* Cambridge: Harvard Univ. Press, 1935.

Illinois in 1837. Philadelphia: S. A. Mitchell, 1837.

Johnston, J. Stoddard. *Memorial History of Louisville.* Chicago: American Biographical Publishing Co., 1896.

Lazarus, Emma. *Poems.* 2 vols. Boston: Houghton Mifflin, 1889.

McGill, F. T. "Thoreau and College Discipline," *New England Quarterly,* XV (June, 1942), 349–53.

Marquand, John P. "A Hearsay History of Curzon's Mill," *Atlantic,* CC (November, 1957), 84–91.

Morison, Samuel Eliot. *By Land and by Sea.* New York: Knopf, 1953.

———. "Edward Channing, a Memoir," *Proceedings of the Massachusetts Historical Society,* LXVI (1931), 434–38.

———. *Three Centuries of Harvard.* Cambridge: Harvard Univ. Press, 1937.

New Bedford *Daily Mercury,* 1856 *passim.*

New York *Evening Post,* March 4, 5, 1846.

Pierce, E. L. *Memoir and Letters of Charles Sumner.* Boston: Roberts Brothers, 1877.

Poe, Edgar Allan. *Complete Works,* ed. James A. Harrison. 17 vols. New York: Crowell, 1902.

———. "Our Amateur Poets," *Graham's Magazine,* XXIII (August, 1843). Partially reprinted in *Southern Literary Messenger,* XVI (October, 1850), 610–12.

Poor, Mary W. "Recollections of Brookline," *Publications of the Brookline* [Mass.] *Historical Society,* 1903.

Ricketson, Anna and Walton. *Daniel Ricketson and His Friends.* Boston and New York: Houghton Mifflin, 1902.

Rusk, Ralph Leslie. *Life of Ralph Waldo Emerson.* New York: Scribner, 1949.

Sanborn, Franklin B. "The Friendships of Hawthorne," *Hawthorne Centenary Celebration at the Wayside, July 4–7, 1904.* Boston: Houghton Mifflin, 1905.

———. *The Life of Henry David Thoreau.* Boston: Houghton Mifflin, 1917.

———. *Recollections of Seventy Years.* 2 vols. Boston: Gorham, 1909.

———. "William Ellery Channing and Daniel Ricketson," New Bedford *Mercury,* August 7, 1907.

Silver, Rollo G. "Ellery Channing's Collaboration with Emerson," *American Literature,* VII (March, 1935), 84–86.

Stern, Madeleine B. "Four Letters from George Keats," *PMLA,* LVI (March, 1941), 207–18.

Stewart, Randall. *Nathaniel Hawthorne: A Biography.* New Haven: Yale Univ. Press, 1948.

Thoreau, Henry David. *Correspondence,* ed. Walter Harding and Carl Bode. New York: New York Univ. Press, 1958.

———. *The Journal of Henry D. Thoreau,* ed. Bradford Torrey and Francis H. Allen. 14 vols. in 2. New York: Dover Publications, 1962.

———. *Walden.* Boston and New York: Houghton Mifflin, 1902.

Ticknor, George. *The Life, Letters, and Journals of George Ticknor,* ed. Ferris Greenslet. 2 vols. Boston: Houghton Mifflin, 1909.

Woodberry, George. *Edgar Allan Poe.* Boston: Houghton Mifflin, 1885.

Woods, Harriet F. *Historical Sketches of Brookline, Mass.* Boston: Privately printed, 1874.

Ybarra, T. R. *Young Man of Caracas.* New York: I. Washburn, 1941.

Index

Frederick T. McGill Jr.

Professor McGill grew up in Massachusetts, familiar with the Concord tradition and much interested in the Puritan heritage and what we have done with it. During the summers he and Mrs. McGill help run the Star Island Conference Center on the Isles of Shoals off the New Hampshire coast, where the writers of Cambridge and Boston gathered in the 1870s and '80s and now Unitarians and Congregationalists meet to discuss ethical problems ranging from international relations to the relationships between parents and children.

He secured his bachelor's and master's degrees from Harvard, then took a teaching position at what has become the Newark College of Rutgers, the State University. Now Professor of English and Associate Dean, he teaches a course on Emerson, Thoreau, and Hawthorne which he calls "The Concord Group."